Awa' an' Bile yer Heid!

Scottish Curses and Insults

Compiled and edited by

David Ross

Birlinn

First published in 1999 by
Birlinn Limited
West Newington House
10 Newington Road
Edinburgh
EH9 1QS

www. birlinn.co.uk

Reprinted October 1999
New edition 2002

ISBN 1 84158 244 1

British Library Cataloguing-in-Publication Data
A catalogue record for this book is available
from the British Library

Typeset by Textype, Cambridge
Printed and bound in Great Britain by
Cox & Wyman Ltd, Reading

CONTENTS

Introduction..v
Animals...1
Architecture and Buildings 2
Art and Artists...3
Authors..5
Clothes and Fashion...13
Curses, Imprecations and Visions...15
Edinburgh vs Glasgow...20
England and the English 20
Entertainment..23
Epitaphs 28
Fictional Insults...36
Food, Drink and Hospitality 40
Glossary of Insulting Terms 45
Government...46
Internecine Insults...47
Jibes and Put-Downs 56
Judgements of Various Kinds 57
The Kirk, God and the Devil 77
The Land 88
The Languages...90
The Law 93
Manners 96
Medicine, Hygiene and Doctors 97
Men 98
Personalities...100
Places 112
Politics and Politicians..122
Repartee 133
Royalty, Lords, Lairds and Ladies...137
Schools and Universities..147
Scotland, as seen by Others 148
Scots, as seen by Others 150
Sports 157
Traditions and Festivities...161
Travel and Transport...162
Warfare 163
Wives and Husbands...164
Women...166
Great Insulters 171

Index of Authors Quoted 180

She's a classy girl, though, at least all her tattoos are spelt right – *Chic Murray*

INTRODUCTION

'Treat with scornful abuse' says the *Concise Oxford Dictionary* for 'insult'. 'Abuse, hearty abuse, is a tonic to all save men of indifferent health,' wrote Norman Douglas in the preface to his collection of rude limericks. The best insult, though, occupies an indefinite space between wit and abuse. It contains elements of both to varying degree. A successful insult might provoke laughter in the uncommitted bystander or reader, but it must sting its victim, or it is a failure.

Clever insults are even rarer than good jokes. The rarest of all are instant verbal shafts, created and delivered in a flash of angry inspiration. These are naturally also the most difficult to track down. Many go unrecorded, or are hard to verify. Others are 'improved' in the passing on.

Not all the content of this book, whilst undeniably offensive to its wide range of targets, can be called insult in the strict sense. But if it is not insult, it is definitely invective, defined in the *Concise Oxford Dictionary* as 'violent attack in words'. The lack of scorn is more than compensated for by the presence of rage, indignation, humour and imaginative composition.

The Scots, a small nation adjacent to a large one, learned the art of international insult early. Scots–English relations provided a rich ground for abuse, particularly at times of stress and warfare, which were a very great deal of the time up to and indeed after 1707. Indeed, the intense debate that preceded and accompanied the Treaty of Union in 1707 produced some of the most bitter invective from both sides, perhaps only exceeded in Scotland by the abuse exchanged by fellow-Christians of different sects.

But however soft and attractive the target on the other side of the Border, it has never distracted the Scots from insulting one another. A sense of internal rivalry and competition has always been present in Scotland, expressed in a host of local exchanges. When such things as Sunday School Picnic outings used to occur, the escorting adults, on this day of juvenile liberty, had to close their ears to loud chants of un-neighbour-loving abuse from the top deck of the double decker bus as it went slowly through adjacent villages:

'Beauly rats are scared of cats,
Doo-dah, doo-dah,'

would chant the children of Muir of Ord, and the compliment would be duly paid back when it was Beauly's turn to go on a trip. Even within a community, excuses can always be found to take sides. 'Uppies' and 'Doonies' in Kirkwall meet in ritual struggle each New Year's day. The ultimate manifestation of this intra-mural opposition occurs in football with the Glaswegian confrontations of the 'Old Firm' of Rangers and Celtic, which do not always stop at the purely verbal level. But insults in Scotland have always been delivered at the maker's own risk. At one time, the risk was officially a capital one. In the reign of James VI, a Scot, Thomas Ross, had his right hand struck off and then was beheaded at the Cross of Edinburgh for publishing (in England) a Latin thesis advocating the removal from England of all Scotsmen (except the King, 'his sons, and ane verrie few otheris').

There is often a forceful quality to the Scottish mind which encourages 'Flyting'. This art form, vigorously practised during the fifteenth and early sixteenth centuries, was essentially an exchange of more or less poetically arranged abuse, far more concerned with personality than argument. Even the kings might participate, which sheds some light on the relationships within the small and intimate Scottish court.

That is not to say that the Scots are world leaders in the matter of insult. Our numbers are too small, our circumstances too restricted. We have done creditably in a small compass, but never quite attained that simmeringly over-ripe stage of high-bred civilisation, suave perfection of social manners, and thinly-veiled political corruption, combining to produce an atmosphere which encourages the most subtly barbed offensiveness. The French, the English, even the latter-day New Yorkers, all have had a richer field to pluck from.

This collection also covers insults to Scotland and the Scots. Possibly to the surprise of the inhabitants, not all those who entered the country, or encountered its citizens, became enthusiasts. The Scots have never taken kindly to hostile judgements by strangers. In the early seventeenth century, King James VI spent the then very large sum of £600 to procure the killing in Poland of one Stercovius, a Pole, who, having had a rough reception in Scotland, had had the temerity to compose a satire on the Scots. James tried unsuccessfully to get the Scottish burghs to repay his expenditure. Stercovius' text, like that of the above-mentioned Thomas Ross, is lost.

The most essential thing about insults is that they should be real. Whether spoken or written, they should have been fired, with a will to damage, by an individual. But the balm of time soothes old sores, and as the purpose of this collection is to entertain, there are only one or two examples of the rancid hate that still lurks under certain stones. There is also a section of insults from fiction and drama, created in the single brain of an author, and aimed by an imaginary character at an imaginary target.

And so, happy reading, or browsing. If you don't like it, 'Awa' an' bile yer heid!'

ANIMALS

Ye ugly, creepin, blasted wonner,
Detested, shunn'd by saint and sinner,
How daur ye set your fit upon her –
Sae fine a lady?
Gae somewhere else, and seek your dinner
On some poor body.

Robert Burns (1759–1796), To a Louse

The confounded fleas of mischief and grief . . .
If I could round you all up and stow you in a barrel
And were I blessed with the means I'd send you to Adolf,
Mixed with body-hugging crablice and bugs from the rugs
I'd have it poured about his skull and he'd be locked in his
room.

Angus Campbell (1903–82), The Fleas of Poland, *from*
Gaelic

Of all forms of life, surely the most vile. The cleg was
silent, the colour of old horse manure, a sort of living ghost
of evil.

Neil M. Gunn (1891–1973), on the cleg, in Highland River

That the dogs are lousy is not to be wondered at, since so
many of the islanders themselves spend their entire lives in
that unsavoury condition.

Alasdair Alpin MacGregor, The Western Isles *(1949)*

ARCHITECTURE AND BUILDINGS

The Armadillo

Local name for the entrance hall of the Auditorium at the Scottish Exhibition & Conference Centre, Glasgow

During a tour of New York, A. J. Balfour was shown over one of the city's tallest and most recent skyscrapers. He was told how much it had cost to build, how many men had been employed in its construction, how long it had taken to build, and how fast the lifts travelled.
'Dear me, how remarkable,' he murmured. Finally his guide informed him that the building was so solid that it would easily last for a thousand years.
'Dear, dear me, what a great pity.'

Noted of Arthur James Balfour (1848–1930), in K. Williams, Acid Drops *(1980)*

From my window I see the rectangular blocks of man's
Insolent mechanical ignorance rise, with hideous exactitude,
against the sun
against the sky.
It is the University.

Alan Jackson (1938–), From My Window

. . . the ceilings are so low all you can have for tea is kippers.

Comment on bungalows, recorded in Charles MacKean, The Scottish Thirties

Day by day, one new villa, one new object of offence, is added to another; all around Newington and Morningside, the dismallest structures keep springing up like mushrooms; the pleasant hills are loaded with them, each impudently squatted in its garden ... They belong to no style of art, only to a form of business.

Robert Louis Stevenson (1850–1894), Picturesque Notes on Edinburgh

At last I view the storied scene,
The embattled rock and valley green;
And hear, mid reverent nature's hush,
The water closet's frequent flush.

John Warrack, letter to The Scotsman *protesting against the building of a public lavatory in Princes Street Gardens, Edinburgh (December 1920)*

It is worse than ridiculous to see the people of Dumfries coming forward with their pompous mausoleum.

William Wordsworth (1770–1850), Letter to John Scott (1816), on the Burns tomb in Dumfries

Those sunless courts, entered by needles' eyes of apertures, congested with hellish, heaven-scaling barracks, reeking with refuse and evil odours, inhabited promiscuously by poverty and prostitution.

Israel Zangwill on Edinburgh tenements (1895)

ART AND ARTISTS

May the Devil fly away with the fine arts!

Thomas Carlyle (1795–1881), Latter-Day Pamphlets

... many of these artists in this exhibition seem to have an overt and blatant concern with money and, inevitably, status. They have dramatically reduced the scope and vision of their art so that it may become a saleable commodity, a potential piece of private property and a casual investment for Scotland's doomed and essentially philistine bourgeoisie.

Ken Currie, reviewing the exhibition 'Contemporary Art from Scotland' in Stigma 2 *(1983)*

Arts Councils are the insane asylums of bureaucracy.

Ian Hamilton Finlay, 'An Alphabet', Studio International (1981)

. . . the unfortunate monarch, whose head was executed as ruthlessly on canvas as she herself had been at Fotheringay.

H. Grey Graham, The Social Life of Scotland in the Eighteenth Century (1899), on posthumous portraits of Mary, Queen of Scots

'My dear Roberts,' wrote the critic in a private letter, 'you may have seen my remarks on your pictures. I hope they will make no difference to our friendship. Yours, etc.'
'My dear — ,' wrote the painter in reply, 'the next time I meet you I shall pull your nose. I hope it will make no difference to our friendship. Yours, etc., D. Roberts.'

Told of David Roberts (1796–1864) in Alexander Hislop, The Book of Scottish Anecdote (1883)

AUTHORS

It is really very generous of Mr Thomson to consent to live at all.

Anonymous contemporary critic of James Thomson (1834–1882), poet of voluptuous death, quoted in notes to Douglas Young, Scottish Verse 1851–1951 *(1952)*

'You ought to be roasted alive, though even then you would not be to my taste.'

Sir J.M. Barrie (1860–1937), to George Bernard Shaw, quoted in K. Williams, Acid Drops, *1980*

Why bother yourself about the cataract of drivel for which Conan Doyle was responsible?

Joseph Bell (1837–1911), said to have been Conan Doyle's model for Sherlock Holmes, in a letter

'It adds a new terror to death.'

Lord Brougham (1778–1868), Lord Chancellor of Great Britain, on Lord Campbell's Lives of the Lord Chancellors *(1845–47)*

O thou whom poesy abhors,
Whom prose has turned out of doors!
Heardst thou that groan?
Proceed no farther:
'Twas laurelled Martial roaring murther.

Robert Burns (1759–1796), on James Elphinston's (1721–1809) translation of Martial's Epigrams

And think'st thou, Scott! by vain conceit perchance,

On public taste to foist thy stale romance . . .
No! when the sons of song descend to trade,
Their bays are sear, their former laurels fade.
Let such forgo the poet's sacred name,
Who rack their brains for lucre, not for fame.

Lord Byron (1788–1824), English Bards and Scotch
Reviewers, *on Sir Walter Scott*

Fricassee of dead dog . . . A truly unwise little book. The
kind of man that Keats was gets ever more horrible to me.
Force of hunger for pleasure of every kind, and want of all
other force – such a soul, it would once have been very
evident, was a chosen 'vessel of Hell'.

Thomas Carlyle (1795–1881), on Monckton Milnes's Life
of Keats

A weak, diffusive, weltering, ineffectual man . . . Never did
I see such apparatus got ready for thinking, and so little
thought. He mounts scaffolding, pulleys and tackle, gathers
all the tools in the neighbourhood with labour, with noise,
demonstration, precept, abuse, and sets – three bricks.

Thomas Carlyle, on Samuel Taylor Coleridge

A more pitiful, rickety, gasping, staggering, stammering
Tomfool I do not know. Poor Lamb! Poor England! when
such a despicable abortion is given the name of genius.

Thomas Carlyle, on Charles Lamb

Shelley is a poor creature, who has said or done nothing
worth a serious man being at the trouble of remembering.

Thomas Carlyle, on Percy Bysshe Shelley

At bottom, this Macaulay is but a poor creature with his

dictionary literature and erudition, his saloon arrogance. He has no vision in him. He will neither see nor do any great thing.

Thomas Carlyle, on Lord Macaulay

. . . standing in a cess-pool, and adding to it

Thomas Carlyle on Algernon Charles Swinburne (1837–1909), quoted in Jean Overton Fuller, Swinburne (1968)

All his life he loved attempting magnificent things in a slapdash way and, whatever others might think, he was seldom dissatisfied with the result.

Donald Carswell on J.S. Blackie, in Brother Scots *(1927)*

Joanna Baillie is now almost totally forgotten, even among feminist academics dredging the catalogues for third-rate women novelists . . . Her life story is a quaint one, interesting for being so dull.

Rupert Christiansen, Romantic Affinities *(1988), on the 19th century tragedian Joanna Baillie*

. . . to conclude, they say in few words
That Gilbert is not worth two cow turds,
Because when he has crack't so crouse,
His mountains just bring forth a mouse.

Samuel Colville, Pindarique Ode on Bishop Burnet's 'Dialogues', *c. 1689. Gilbert Burnet (1643–1715) became Bishop of Salisbury under William of Orange and was detested by both Presbyterians and Jacobites*

The man's mind was not clean . . . he degraded and prostituted his intellect, and earned thereby the love and worship of a people whose distinguishing trait is fundamental lewdness ... Put into decent English many of his most vaunted lays amount to nothing at all ... His life as a whole would have discredited a dustman, much less a poet ... a superincontinent yokel with a gift for metricism.

T.W. Crosland, The Unspeakable Scot *(1902), on Robert Burns (and his fellow-countrymen)*

For blithering sentiment of the cheapest and most obvious sort, these personages have certainly never been equalled ... creatures of a sentiment so slobbery that it would be eschewed even by the scribbling, simpering, misses at a seminary.

T.W. Crosland, The Unspeakable Scot, *on Sir J.M. Barrie's 'Thrums' stories*

... deplorable is the mildest epithet one can justly apply to it. Wordsworth writes somewhere of a person 'who would peep and botanise about his mother's grave'. This is exactly the feeling that a reading of *Margaret Ogilvy* gives you.

T.W. Crosland, The Unspeakable Scot, *on Sir J.M. Barrie's memoir of his mother*

Mr Coleridge was in bad health; – the particular reason is not given; but the careful reader will form his own conclusions ... Upon the whole, we look upon this publication as one of the most notable pieces of impertinence of which the press has lately been guilty.

The Edinburgh Review, *anonymous review of Samuel Taylor Coleridge's* Kubla Khan *(1816)*

On Waterloo's ensanguined plain
Lie tens of thousands of the slain;
But none, by sabre or by shot,

Fell half so flat as Walter Scott.

Thomas, Lord Erskine (1750–1823), on Sir Walter Scott's The Field of Waterloo

It is a story of crofter life near Stonehaven; but it is questionable if the author, or authoress, is correct in the description of crofter girls' underclothing of that period.

Fife Herald *book review, quoted in L.G. Gibbon and Hugh MacDiarmid, Scottish Scene (1934)*

The bleatings of a sheep.

John Fraser, Professor of Celtic at Oxford University, on the translations from Gaelic of Kenneth Macleod (1871–1955), quoted in The Memoirs of Lord Bannerman of Kildonan

Mr Gunn is a brilliant novelist from Scotshire who chooses his home county as the scene of his tales. . . he is the greatest loss to itself that Scottish literature has suffered in this century.

Lewis Grassic Gibbon (James Leslie Mitchell, 1901–35), Scottish Scene

wee Maurice (most minuscule of makars)

Hamish Henderson (1920–2002) on Maurice Lindsay, letter to Hugh MacDiarmid, 3 April 1949

The final word on Burns must always be that he is the least rewarding of his country's major exports, neither so nourishing as porridge, or stimulating as whisky, nor so relaxing as golf.

Kenneth Hopkins, English Poetry, *quoted in Hugh MacDiarmid,* Lucky Poet *(1943)*

If you imagine a Scotch commercial traveller in a Scotch commercial hotel leaning on the bar and calling the barmaid *Dearie*, then you will know the keynote of Burns's verse.

A.E. Housman (1859–1936), quoted in Jonathon Green, Dictionary of Insulting Quotations *(1996)*

Dr Donne's verses are like the Peace of God, for they pass all understanding.

King James VI (1566–1625), attributed, on the poems of John Donne

This will never do!

Lord Jeffrey (1773–1850), reviewing Wordsworth's The Excursion *in* The Edinburgh Review, *November 1814*

This, we think, has the merit of being the very worst poem we ever saw imprinted in a quarto volume.

Lord Jeffrey, reviewing Wordsworth's The White Doe of Rylstone, *in* The Edinburgh Review, *October 1815*

'Writers are too difficult.'

A member of the Glasgow Festivals Unit team, on why so few writers were involved in the city's 'Culture Year' (1990), quoted in James Kelman, Some Recent Attacks *(1992)*

'Yuh wrote? A po-it? Micht ye no' juist as weel hae peed inti thuh wund?'

Maurice Lindsay (1918–) recalling the comment of an anonymous Glaswegian 'In a Glasgow Loo', from Robin Bell, The Best of Scottish Poetry *(1989)*

Does she, poor silly thing, pretend
The manners of our age to mend?

Mad as we are, we're wise enough
Still to despise sic paultry stuff.

Janet Little (1751–1813), 'Given to a Lady Who Asked Me To Write a Poem'

. . . calm, settled, imperturbable drivelling idiocy . . . We will venture to make one small prophecy, that his bookseller will not a second time venture £50 on any thing he can write. It is a better and a wiser thing to be a starved apothecary than a starved poet; so back to the shop, Mr John, back to 'plasters, pills, and ointment boxes, etc.'.

J.G. Lockhart (1794–1854) in Blackwood's Magazine, *1818, on John Keats's* Endymion

Servile and impertinent, shallow and pedantic, a bigot and a sot, bloated with family pride, and eternally blustering about the dignity of a born gentleman, yet stooping to be a talebearer, and eavesdropper, a common butt in the taverns of London . . . Everything which another man would have hidden, everything the publication of which would have made another man hang himself, was matter of exaltation to his weak and diseased mind.

Lord Macaulay (1800–1859), on James Boswell (1740–1795)

high-falutin' nonsense,
Spiritual masturbation of the worst sort.

Hugh MacDiarmid (C.M. Grieve, 1892–1978), on the 'Celtic Twilight' works of 'Fiona Macleod' (William Sharp, 1856–1905)

I remember well when Mr Lindsay first climbed on to the bandwagon of the Scottish Renaissance Movement. He came to see me about it. I had no difficulty whatever in appreciating that under his natty khaki shirt what may be described as his bosom was warming with the glowing ecstasy of a dog sighting a new and hitherto undreamed-of lamp-post.

Hugh MacDiarmid (C.M. Grieve, 1892–1978), A Soldier's Farewell to Maurice Lindsay, *in* National Weekly, *June 1952. (Lindsay had criticised MacDiarmid's introduction to a Scottish concert at the Institute of Contemporary Arts, London)*

Calf-fighter Campbell . . .
there's an operation to do first
– To remove the haemorrhoids you call your poems

Hugh MacDiarmid, on Roy Campbell, the South African poet

There was another old lady who knew and loved the songs of the bard William Ross. This particular morning she spent singing William Ross's songs behind closed doors. A pious neighbour overheard her beautiful singing . . . She came in later and said. 'Yours was the beautiful singing this morning. Surely it was the Psalms of David that you sang.' 'David, the excremental blackguard!' replied the other. 'What good was he compared to William Ross?'

Calum Maclean, The Highlands of Scotland

He is writing a novel and his characters all want soaking in double strong disinfectant for a week.

Rhea Mitchell, wife of Lewis Grassic Gibbon, in a letter of March 1927 about his first novel, Stained Radiance

For thee, James Boswell, may the hand of Fate
Arrest thy goose-quill and confine thy prate!

. . . To live in solitude, oh! be thy luck,
A chattering magpie on the Isle of Muck.

Peter Pindar (John Wolcott, 1738–1819), Bozzy and Piozzi

She has dedicated her menopause to me.

*Muriel Spark (1918–) on an American editor who criticised
her autobiography,* Curriculum Vitae

the most foul-mouthed man of genius since the death of
Swift.

Algernon Charles Swinburne (1837–1909), Note on the
Muscovite Crusade, *on Thomas Carlyle*

As artists we situate ourselves at the level of man-at-crap.

*Alexander Trocchi (1925–1984), quoted in Andrew Murray
Scott,* Alexander Trocchi: The Making of the Monster *(1991)*

CLOTHES AND FASHION

A' our town needlers are growing sae grand,
That strangers would tak' them for ladies o' land,
With their fine silken gowns and their black satin bags,
But mark what's below them is naething but rags.

Anonymous, The Dandies of Deception, c. *1830, on the
town-girls of Scotland*

The common habit of the ordinary Highlanders is far from
being acceptable to the eye . . . this dress is called the *quelt;*
and for the most part, they wear the petticoat so very short,
that in a windy day, going up a hill, or stooping, the
indecency of it is plainly discovered.

Edmund Burt (c. 1695–1755), Letters from a Gentleman in the North of Scotland *(1728–37)*

The garb of old Gaul is no doubt very fetching from the point of view of the weak-minded, but of its effeminacy there can be no doubt. Really it is a costume for small and pretty boys who are too young to be breeched.

T.W. Crosland, The Unspeakable Scot *(1902)*

The Hielan' man he wears the kilt, even when it's snowin';
He kens na where the wind comes frae, but he kens fine where it's goin'.

Joe Gordon, The Hielan' Chorus

Cursed be the king who stretched our stockings;
down in the dust may his face be found.

John MacCodrum (c. 1693–1779), Oran Mu'n Eideadh Ghaidealach (Song of the Highland Dress), *on the banning of the kilt and tartan, 1746*

The Gaelic poet Rob Donn Mackay made his first recorded verse when he was still only four or five, objecting to the frock in which small boys used to be clad until old enough to assume kilt or breeches:

I'm not to blame – the tailor is,
A blundering fool was he,
That buttons put behind my back,
Where I had not eyes to see.

Rob Donn Mackay (c.1714–1778), from Gaelic

Wi' shanks like that ye'd better hae stuck to breeks!

Charles Murray (1864–1941), Ay, Fegs – *call from the crowd to a soldier in a kilt*

This tartan obsession – prior to Walter Scott the average clan gathering looked like a parade of tattie bags.

W. Gordon Smith, Mr Jock *(1987)*

CURSES, IMPRECATIONS AND VISIONS

The curse of hell frae me sall ye bear,
Mither, mither;
The curse of hell frae me sall ye bear,
Sic counsels ye gave to me, O.

Anonymous, Edward

O bonny balms come tell to me
What kind o' a daith I'll hae to dee?
Seven years a fish in the flood,
Seven years a bird in the wood.
Seven years a tongue to the warnin' bell,
And seven long years in the flames o' hell

Anonymous, The Cruel Mother

Curse Thou his basket and his store,
Kail an' potatoes.

Robert Burns (1759–1796), Holy Willie's Prayer

Curs'd be the man, the poorest wretch in life,
The crouching vassal to a tyrant wife!

Robert Burns, The Henpecked Husband

O Fergusson! thy glorious parts
Ill suited law's dry, musty arts!
My curse upon your whunstane hearts,

Ye E'nbrugh gentry!
The tythe o' what ye waste at cartes
Wad stow'd his pantry!

Robert Burns, Epistle To William Simson, *referring to the poet Robert Fergusson (1750–1774)*

First on the head of him who did this deed
My curse shall light, – on him and all his seed:
Without one spark of intellectual fire,
Be all the sons as senseless as the sire:
If one with wit the parent brood disgrace,
Believe him bastard of a brighter race.

Lord Byron (1788–1824), The Curse of Minerva, *on Lord Elgin (1766–1841), remover of the Parthenon sculptures from Athens to London*

I curse their head and all the hairs of their head, I curse their face, their eyes, their mouth, their nose, their tongue, their teeth, their shoulders, their backs and their heart . . . Before and behind, within and without. I curse them walking and I curse them riding. I curse them standing and I curse them sitting . . . I dissever and part them from the Kirk of God, and deliver them quick to the devill of Hell.

Curse issued by Archbishop Dunbar of Glasgow, early 16th century, against those who break the laws of the Church, quoted in George Blake, Scottish Treasure Trove *(c. 1930)*

I denounce, proclaimis and declaris all and sundry the committaris of the said saikles murthris, slauchteris, brinying, herirchippen, reiffs, thiftis and spulezies . . . and their counsalouris and defendouris of thair evil deeds generalie CURSIT, waryit aggregeite, and reaggregaite, with the GREIT CURSING . . . All the malesouns and waresouns that ever gat warldlie creature sen the begynnyng of the warlde to this hour mot licht upon thaim. The maledictioun of God, that lichtit apon Lucifer and all his fallows, that strak them frae the hie hevin to the deep hell, mot licht apon thaim . . . And their candillis gangis frae your sicht, as mot their saulis gang frae the visage of God, and thair gude faim fra the warld, quhile thai forbeir thair oppin synnis foirsaid, and rise frae this terribill cursing, and mak satisfactioun and pennance.

Curse pronounced by Archbishop Gavin Douglas of Glasgow on the Border Reivers, c. 1625, quoted in George Macdonald Fraser, The Steel Bonnets *(1971)*

'De'il colic the wame o' thee, thou false thief! Dost thou say mass at my lug?'

Saying attributed to Jenny Geddes, Edinburgh stallkeeper, on the occasion of the first attempt to read from Archbishop Laud's Liturgy in St Giles Cathedral (as it then was), 23 July 1637

Son of a Scots manse though you were
I've taken the rare scunner against you,
You who thieve the golden hours of bairns,
You who bitch up the world's peoples
With crystal images, pitch-black lies,
You who have ended civilised conversation
And dished out licences to print banknotes,
May your soul shrink to the size of a midge
And never rest in a couthie kirkyard
But dart across a million wee screens
And be harassed by TV jingles for ever and ever,
For thine's the kingdom of the *televisor*,
You goddam bloody genius, John Logie Baird!

Robert Greacen, Curse

Fra heat of body I thee now deprive,
And to thy sickness sall be na recure,

Bot in dolour thy dayis to endure.
Thy crystal ene minglit with blude I mak;
Thy voice so clear unpleasand, hoir and hace;

Thy lusty lire ourspersed with spottis black,
And lumpis haw appearand in thy face.

Robert Henryson (c. 1425–c. 1500), the curse of leprosy put on Cressida, from The Testament of Cresseid

That d — d Sir Walter Scott, that everybody makes such a work about! ... I wish I had him to ferry over Loch Lomond: I should be after sinking the boat, if I drowned myself into the bargain; for ever since he wrote his *Lady of the Lake,* as they call it, everybody goes to see that filthy hole Loch Katrine, then comes round by Luss, and I have had only two gentlemen to guide all this blessed season.

Loch Lomond ferryman, after publication of Scott's Lady of the Lake *in 1810*

Curse his new hoose, his business, his cigar,
His wireless set, and motor car,
Alsatian, gauntlet gloves, plus-fours and wife,
— A' thing included in his life;
And, abune a', his herty laughter,
And, if he has yin, his hereafter.

Hugh MacDiarmid (C.M. Grieve, 1892–1978), Thoughts On My Boss

My malison light ilka day,
On them that drink and dinna pay.

Allan Ramsay (1686–1758), Lucky Spence's Last Advice

Fyvie, Fyvie, thou's ne'er thrive ye
As lang as in thee there's stanis three:
There's ane intil the highest tower,
There's ane intil the ladye's bower,
There's ane aneath the water yett,
And thir three stanis ye'se never get!

Thomas the Rhymer (fl. 14th century), Curse Upon Fyvie
Castle

Ugie, Ugie by the sea,
Lordless shall thy landis be,
And underneath thy hearthstane,
The tod shall bring her bairnis hame.

Thomas the Rhymer, Curse Upon the Earl Marischal's
Castle

High though his titles, proud his name,
Boundless his wealth as wish can claim, –
Despite those titles, power and pelf

The wretch, concentred all in self,
Living, shall forfeit fair renown,

And doubly dying shall go down
To the vile dust from whence he sprung,
Unwept, unhonoured and unsung.

Sir Walter Scott (1771–1832), The Lay of the Last Minstrel

May William, the son of George, be as a leafless splintered
tree, rootless, branchless, sproutless. May there be no joy on
his hearth, no wife, no brother, no son, no sounding harp or
blazing wax.

John Roy Stuart (fl. 18th century), Curse Upon the Duke of
Cumberland, *after Culloden, 1746, from Gaelic*

Fuck off, ya plukey-faced wee hing-oot.

Irvine Welsh (1957–), Trainspotting

EDINBURGH vs GLASGOW

' . . . all the wise men in Glasgow come from the East –
that's to say, they come from Edinburgh.'
'Yes, and the wiser they are, the quicker they come.'

Neil Munro (1864–1930), Erchie, My Droll Friend

One day, when I was taking tea with a well-known Scottish
divine in Glasgow, the conversation turned on Edinburgh,
its charm, its menace, its appeal. Suddenly my companion
leant forward over the table, a strange gleam in his eyes.
'They say there are more amateur tarts in Edinburgh than
anywhere else,' he said, with a grave intensity.

George Malcolm Thomson, The Re-Discovery of Scotland
(1928)

ENGLAND AND THE ENGLISH

It was an ancient conceit of the Scots to pretend that the
English were born with tails. In one of the legends of
William Wallace, his famous confrontation with the
English soldiers in Lanark (1296) began when he protected
a small boy who had put his fingers behind his back and
waggled them like a tail at the angry pikemen.

To save a maid St George a dragon slew,
A brave exployt if all that's said is true,
Some think there are no dragons; nay, 'tis said

There was no George; pray God there was a maid.

Anonymous lines on England's patron saint, 18th century, from J. Maidment, Book of Scottish Pasquils (1866)

Why do we always get Julians and Timothys? Let's get some Wullies in charge.

Anonymous protest against the appointment of an Englishman as Director of the National Galleries of Scotland, quoted in A. Cran and J. Robertson, Dictionary of Scottish Quotations (1996)

He is an egregious dissembler and a great liar. Away with him, he is a greeting divil.

Robert Blair (1593–166), on Oliver Cromwell, quoted in Thomas McCrie, The Life of Mr Robert Blair (1848)

. . . when I humour any of them in an outrageous contempt of Scotland, I fairly own I treat them as children. And thus I have, at some moments, found myself obliged to treat even Dr Johnson.

James Boswell (1740–95), Journal of a Tour to the Hebrides

. . . for the most part the worst instructed, and the the least knowing of their rank, I ever went amongst.

Gilbert Burnet (1643–1715), History of His Own Times, on the English aristocracy

Thirty millions, mostly fools.

Thomas Carlyle (1795–1881), when asked what the population of England was

Even a boiled egg tastes of mutton fat in England.

Norman Douglas (1868–1952), Old Calabria

The Englishman remains everlastingly adolescent.

Norman Douglas, Old Calabria

Let bragart England in disdain
Ha'd ilka lingo, but her ain:
Her ain, we wat, say what she can,
Is like her true-born Englishman,
A vile promiscuous mungrel seed
O' Danish, Dutch an' Norman breed,
An' prostituted since, to a'
The jargons on this earthly ba'!

Alexander Geddes (1737–1802), Epistle to the Society of
Antiquaries

An Englishman is a man who lives on an island in the North
Sea governed by Scotsmen.

Philip Guedalla, Supers and Supermen *(1920)*

. . . if one will only read the anecdotes of village 'loonies'
with which Scots literature abounds . . . he will find that the
average Scots idiot was a creature of considerably more
humour than the average Englishman.

J. A. Hammerton, J. M. Barrie and His Books

The Barbarians who inhabit the banks of the Thames

David Hume (1711–1776), letter to Hugh Blair, April 1764

I hate London, and I do not think that either flattery or profit can ever make me love it.

James Hogg (1770–1835), letter to his wife, January 1832

Sir, it is not so much to be lamented that Old England is lost, as that the Scotch have found it.

Samuel Johnson (1709–1784), to James Boswell, 15 May 1776

Boswell was praising the English highly, and saying they were a fine, open people. 'Oh –' said Macpherson, 'an open people! their mouths, indeed, are open to gluttony to fill their belly, but I know of no other openness they have.'

James Macpherson (1734–1796), quoted in Charles Rogers, Boswelliana *(1874)*

I am heartily tired of this Land of Indifference and Phlegm where the finer Sensations of the Soul are not felt, and Felicity is held to consist in stupefying Port and overgrown Buttocks of Beef, where Genius is lost, and Taste altogether extinguished.

Tobias Smollett (1721–1771), Letter to Alexander Carlyle, March 1754

ENTERTAINMENT

The music for the occasion was provided by the pipe band of the Queen Victoria School and by the military band of the 2nd Battalion Gordon Highlanders. There was no wind to speak of.

Inadvertent insult from a Perthshire local paper

Once at the Edinburgh Festival, two very genteel elderly local ladies were present at a performance of Shakespeare's *Pericles*, which opened on a stage strewn with mirrored cushions and beaten brass tables. 'Where is it supposed to be?' whispered one. Said the other, reading from the programme, '"Egypt – a brothel in Alexandria."' Declared the first, Och, it's *nothing* like a brothel in Alexandria.'

From Nigel Rees, The Guinness Book of Humorous Anecdotes *(1994)*

I have never had to try to get my act across to a non-English speaking audience, except at the Glasgow Empire.

Arthur Askey (1900–1982), English comedian

Another English artiste, a male impersonator making one of several farewell appearances, also met a hostile uproar as soon as she appeared.
But she had a gallant champion. A tall gent rose from his seat in the front row of the stalls and faced the howling mob.
'Aw, come on,' he appealed to them. 'Gi'e the poor auld coo a chance.'
This unexpected intervention brought a brief period of silence during which the lady artiste walked to the footlights and rebuked the noisy mob with the heartfelt words, 'Thank goodness there's ONE gentleman in the audience.'

Stanley Baxter, Stanley Baxter's Bedside Book of Glasgow Humour *(1986)*

Edmund Burt tells the story of a military officer who added a drummer to complement the piper of his Highland company: 'Now the contest between the drummer and the piper arose about the point of honour, and at length the contention grew exceedingly hot, which the captain having notice of, he called them both before him, and, in the end, decided the matter in favour of the drummer; whereupon the piper remonstrated very warmly. "Achs wuds, sir," says he, "and shall a little rascal, that beats upon a sheepskin, tak the right haund of me, that am a musician?"'

Edmund Burt, Letters from the North of Scotland *(1720–37)*

Such a set of ugly creatures as the Chorus I never did see! I grew so sorry for them, reflecting perhaps that each had a life of her own; that perhaps 'somebody loved that pig'; that, if I had any tears in me at the moment, I would have cried for them all packed there like herrings in a barrel, into one mass of sound.

Jane Welsh Carlyle (1801–1866), on a performance of Handel's Messiah

... they brought in a kind of accordion and my hostess (who was regarded locally as a great musician) began with the utmost gravity to play on it the most atrocious tunes.

Frederic Chopin (1810–1849), on a visit to the Duchess of Hamilton, quoted in T. Ratcliffe Barnet, Scottish Pilgrimage in the Land of Lost Content *(1949)*

Jocky, whose manly high–boned cheeks to crown,
With freckles spotted, flamed the golden down,
With meikle art could on the bagpipes play
E'en from the rising to the setting day;
Sawney as long without remorse could bawl
Home's madrigals and ditties from *Fingal*.

Charles Churchill (1731–1764), The Prophecy of Famine

To an artiste, applause is like a banquet ... Thanks for the cheese sandwich.

Billy Connolly (1942–), to a Glasgow audience

Last time I saw a mouth like yours, pal, Lester Piggott was sitting behind it.

Billy Connolly, quoted in D. Campbell, Billy Connolly: The Authorised Version *(1976), to a heckler*

Fair hellish.

Donald Dewar (1937–2000), first First Minister of Scotland, on some Edinburgh Festival Fringe shows, 1999

At the first performance of *Douglas,* when young Norval was busy giving out one of his rodomantading speeches, a canny Scot, who had been observed to grow more and more excited as the piece progressed, unable to contain his feelings, called out with evident pride, 'Whaur's yer Wully Shakespeare noo?'

James C. Dibdin, Annals of the Edinburgh Stage *(1888) referring to the first performance of John Home's play, in Edinburgh, December 1756*

The House of Terror

Ken Dodd, English comedian, referring to the Glasgow Empire theatre, BBC Radio, 8 June 1990

Williamson soon lost patience with a noisy group of young Americans in the audience at a performance of *Macbeth.* He got off his throne, walked down to the footlights, and calmly said, in iambic pentameters:
'If you don't shut your mouths a friend of mine

Will pass among you with a baseball bat.'
Whereupon he adjusted his crown and continued in
complete silence.

Sheila Hancock, Ramblings of an Actress *(1987), on the
actor Nicol Williamson*

Pauper: I will not gif for all your play worth an sowis fart.
Sir David Lindsay (c. 1486–1555), Ane Satyre of The Thrie
Estaitis

How dare anyone discharge, and in the name of singing, the
cacophony to be heard at the popular Gaelic concert?

Alasdair Alpin MacGregor, The Western Isles *(1949)*

Of course, with the kind of people who call Mrs Kennedy-
Fraser's travesties of Gaelic songs 'faithful reproductions of
the spirit of the original' I have no dispute. They are
harmless as long as ignorance and crassness are considered
failings in criticism of poetry.

Sorley Maclean (1911–1996), Criticism and Prose Writings

If fiddling is music, that's enough of it.

*Roderick Morison (An Clàrsair Dall, the Blind Harper,
c. 1655–c. 1714), on hearing a harp tune played on the
fiddle (from Gaelic)*

... that patchwork of blasphemy, absurdity, and gross
obscenity, which the zeal of an early Reformer spawned
under the captivating title of *Ane Compendious Booke of
Godlie and Spirituall Songs* is neither comprehended under
the description of song as we are now in quest of, nor do its
miserable and profane parodies reflect any trace whatsoever
of the stately ancient narrative ballad.

William Motherwell (1797–1835), Introduction to
Minstrelsy Ancient and Modern, *on the Wedderburn
brothers'* Gude and Godlie Ballatis

Put no faith in aught that bears the name of music while you
are in Scotland ... I was asked to a private concert; I
suffered the infliction of several airs with exemplary
patience.

*Amédée Pichot, French consul in Edinburgh, 1822, quoted
in Catherine and Donald Carswell,* The Scots Week-End
(1936)

... the dank euphonies of the Glasgow Orpheus Choir.

Alan Sharp, A Dream of Perfection, *in I. Archer and T.
Royle,* We'll Support You Evermore *(1976)*

I listen to Scottish dance music, as I am immune to it now,
and it doesn't affect me.

*Iain Crichton Smith (1928–), 'Seordag's Interview with the
BBC', by Murdo, in* Thoughts of Murdo

A good taxi-driver wasted.

*A crack (quoted by himself) against Edinburgh comedian
Johnny Victory, whose father ran a taxi business*

EPITAPHS

The 'epitaph' was a favourite form of epigrammatic
character description, either in praise or assassination.
Needless to say, the death of the subject was not necessary
to produce one. The 'bleth'rin bitch' lived on to boast his
fame as a Burnsian victim long after the poet himself was

dead. Burns was an excellent composer of such epitaphs; a few others are also worthy of remembrance.

Here lies a man beside a witch,
Who did oppress both poor and rich;
But whoe he is, or how she fares,
No man doth know, and als few cares.

Here lies my good and gracious Auntie
Whom Death has pack'd in his portmanty,
Three score and ten years did God gift her,
And here she lies: wha' de'il daurs lift her?

Said to have appeared on a tomb in Crail

Beneath this silent tomb is laid
A noisy antiquated maid,
Who from her cradle talked till death
And ne'er before was out of breath.

Epitaph from Dalry, Ayrshire

On a cold pillow lies her head,
Yet it will rise again 'tis said;
So prudently reader how thy walk,
For if she rise again she'll talk.

Epitaph from Biggar

Here lies Mary, the wife of John Ford
We hope her soul is gone to the Lord
But if for Hell she has changed this life
She had better be there than be John Ford's wife.

Epitaph from Potterhill, Paisley

Here lies my wife

A slattern and shrew
If I said I regretted it
I should lie too.

Epitaph from Devonside, Clackmannan

When Orpheus play'd he mov'd Old Nick,
But when you played you made us sick.

Epitaph on a fiddler, said to have been seen in the Mearns

Here lies Tam Reid
Who was chokit to deid
Wi' takin a feed
O' butter and breid
Wi' owre muckle speed,
When he had nae need,
But just for greed.

Epitaph said to have been seen at Cromarty

Here lies an old woman wrapt in her linen,
Mother to James and Thomas Binnen;
Who for want of a coffin was buried in a girnal,
The earth got the shell, and the De'il got the kernel.

Epitaph said to have been seen at Deer, Aberdeenshire

This martyr was by Peter Ingles shot
By birth a Tiger rather than a Scot
Who that his monstrous extract might be seen
Cut off my head and kicked it o'er the Green
Thus was the head which was to wear a crown
A football made by a profane dragoon.

Epitaph of a Covenanter from Fenwick, Ayrshire, 1685

My wife lies here, conveniently,
She is at rest, and so am I.

Said to have been transcribed in a Perthshire graveyard

John Adams lies here o' this parish
A carrier who carried his ale with relish.
He carried so much, he carried so fast,
He could carry no more, so was carried at last:
For the liquor he drank being too much for one
He could carry off, so he's now carrion.

Here continueth to stink
The memory of the Duke of Cumberland
Who with unparalleled barbarity,
And inflexible hardness of heart,
In spite of all motives to lenity
That policy or humanity could suggest,
Endeavoured to ruin Scotland
By all the ways a Tyrant could invent.

*Anonymous Jacobite 'epitaph' for the Duke of Cumberland
after the battle of Culloden, 1746*

Here, Reader, turn your weeping eyes,
My fate a useful moral teaches;
The hole in which my body lies
Would not contain one half my speeches.

*Lines composed on himself by Lord Brougham, sometime
Lord Chancellor (1778–1868)*

Here lyes beneath thir laid-stanes
The carcase of George Glaid-stanes
Wherever be his other half,
Loe here, yee's have his Epitaph.

Anonymous epitaph for George Gladstanes, Archbishop of St Andrews (d. 1615). Row's History of the Kirk *noted: 'He lived a filthie belliegod; he died of a filthie and loathsome disease.'*

Gow and time are even now;
Gow beat time; now Time beats Gow.

Epitaph on Neil Gow, violinist, died 1807

Here lies Mass Andrew Gray,
Of whom no muckle good can I say!
He was ne Quaker, for he had no spirit;
He was ne papist, for he had no merit;
He was ne Turk, for he drank muckle wine;
He was ne Jew, for he eat muckle swine;
Full forty years he preached and le'ed
For which God doomed him when he de'ed.

Epitaph of the Rev. Andrew Gray, Glasgow

Heir layes a lord quho quhill he stood
Had matchless been had he been . . . ;
This Epitaph's a Sylable short,
And ye may add a Sylable to it,
But quhat yat Sylable doeth importe,
My defunct lord could never doe it.

On Thomas Hamilton, Earl of Haddington, died 1637

Within this circular idea
Call'd vulgarly a tomb.
The ideas and impressions lie
That constituted Hume.

Mock epitaph for the sceptical philosopher David Hume (1711–1776), published in A Scotch Haggis *(c. 1820)*

Here continueth to rot
The body of Francis Charteris,
Who, with an Inflexible Constancy and
Inimitable Uniformity of Life
Persisted
In spite of Age and Infirmities
In the practice of Every Human Vice,
Excepting Prodigality and Hypocrisy:
His insatiable Avarice exempted him from the first,
His matchless Impudence from the second.

John Arbuthnot (1667–1735), Epitaph composed for a contemporary

Here lies Boghead among the dead,
In hopes to get salvation;
But if such as he in Heav'n may be,
Then welcome – hail! damnation.

Robert Burns (1759–1796), Epitaph on James Grieve, Laird of Boghead, Tarbolton

Here Souter Hood in death does sleep;
To hell if he's gane thither,
Satan gie him thy gear to keep;
He'll haud it weel thegither.

Robert Burns, Epitaph on a Celebrated Ruling Elder

Below thir stanes lie Jamie's banes;
O Death, it's my opinion,
Thou ne'er took such a bleth'rin bitch
Into thy dark dominion.

Robert Burns, Epitaph on a Noisy Polemic *(James Humphrey, a mason of Mauchline)*

As father Adam first was fool'd
(A case that's still too common),
Here lies a man a woman ruled –
The devil ruled the woman.

Robert Burns, Epitaph on a Henpecked Squire

Lament him, Mauchline husbands a',
He aften did assist ye;
For had ye staid hale weeks awa,
Your wives they ne'er had missed ye.
Ye Mauchline bairns, as on ye press
To school in bands thegither,
O tread you lightly on his grass, –
Perhaps he was your father!

Robert Burns, Epitaph for a Wag in Mauchline *(the poet's friend James Smith)*

Whoe'er thou art, O reader, know
That Death has murder'd Johnie;
An' here his *body* lies fu' low;
For *saul* he ne'er had ony.

Robert Burns, *Epitaph on 'Wee Johnie'* (generally taken to be John Wilson, printer of the first edition of Burns's poems, at Kilmarnock)

Sic a reptile was Wat, a miscreant slave,
That the worms even damned him when laid in his grave;
'In his flesh there's a famine,' a starved reptile cries,
'And his heart is rank poison,' another replies.

Robert Burns, Epitaph for Mr Walter Riddell *(dropped by the Riddell family, Burns took a poet's vengeance)*

Here lies with Death auld Grizel Grim
Lincluden's ugly witch
O Death, how horrid is thy taste
To lie with such a bitch.

Robert Burns, Epitaph for Grizel Grim

Here lies in earth a root of Hell,
Set by the Deil's ain dibble;
This worthless body damn'd himsel,
To save the Lord the trouble.

Robert Burns, Epitaph for D.C., a Suicide

Here lies John Bushby – honest man!
Cheat him, Devil – if you can.

Robert Burns, Epitaph, *on John Bushby, Tinwald Downs*

'Stop thief!' dame Nature call'd to Death,
As Willy drew his latest breath;
'How shall I make a fool again,
My choicest morsel thou hast ta'en.'

Robert Burns, Epitaph, *on William Graham of Mossknowe*

Here lies 'mang ither useless matters,
A. Manson wi' his endless clatters.

Robert Burns, Epitaph on an Innkeeper in Tarbolton,
Andrew Manson (clatters: gossiping)

Here lies a mock-marquis, whose titles were shamm'd,
If he ever rise – it will be to be damn'd.

*Robert Burns, for Mr Marquis, a Dumfries tavern-keeper,
who asked for an epitaph*

In se'enteen hunder'n forty-nine,
The deil gat stuff to make a swine,
An' coost it in a corner;
But wilily he changed his plan,
An' shaped it something like a man,
An' ca'd it Andrew Turner.

Robert Burns, On Andrew Turner

Here lies, of sense bereft –
But sense he never had.
Here lies, by feeling left –
But that is just as bad.
Here lies, reduced to dirt –
That's what he always was.

George Outram (1805–1856), Here Lies

FICTIONAL INSULTS

'My lady, there are few more impressive sights than a
Scotsman on the make.'

Sir J.M. Barrie (1860–1937), What Every Woman Knows

'You've forgotten the grandest moral attribute of a Scotsman,
Maggie, that he'll do nothing which might damage his
career.'

Sir J.M. Barrie, What Every Woman Knows

Oh the gladness of her gladness when she's glad,
And the sadness of her sadness when she's sad;
But the gladness of her gladness,
And the sadness of her sadness
Are as nothing . . .

To the badness of her badness when she's bad.

Sir J.M. Barrie, Rosalind

London! Pompous Ignorance sits enthroned there and welcomes Pretentious Mediocrity with flattery and gifts . . . she entraps great men and sucks their blood.

J.M. Bridie (Osborne Henry Mavor, 1888–1951), The Anatomist

When the Deacon was not afraid of a man he stabbed him straight; when he was afraid of him he stabbed him on the sly.

George Douglas (George Douglas Brown, 1869–1902), The House With the Green Shutters

'Jock Goudie' – an envious bodie will pucker as if he had never heard the name – 'Jock Goudie? Wha's *he* for a Goudie? Oh ay, let me see now. He's a brother o' – eh,' (tit-tit-titting on his brow) – oh, just a brother o' Drucken Will Goudie o' Auchterwheeze! Oo-oh, I ken *him* fine. His grannie keepit a sweetie-shop in Strathbungo.'

George Douglas, The House With the Green Shutters

He dois as dotit dog that damys on all bussis,
And liftis his leg apone loft, thoght he nocht list pische.

William Dunbar (c. 1460–c. 1520), The Tretis of the Twa Marriit Wemen and the Wedow

'Ye're nut on, laddie. Ye're on tae nothin' . . . A gutless wonder like you, that hasn't got the gumption of a louse.'

Archie Hind, The Dear Green Place

'You are, sir, a presumptuous self-conceited pedagogue . . . a mildew, a canker-worm in the bosom of the Reformed Church.

James Hogg (1770–1835), The Private Memoirs and Confessions of a Justified Sinner

'What a wonderful boy he is,' said my mother.
'I'm feared he turn out to be a conceited gowk,' said old Barnet, the minister's man.

James Hogg, The Private Memoirs and Confessions of a Justified Sinner

There was a smug, trim, smooth little minister, making three hundred a year pimping for a God in whom his heart was too small to believe.

Eric Linklater (1899–1974), Magnus Merriman

She looks like a million dollars, but she only knows a hundred and twenty words and she's only got two ideas in her head.

Eric Linklater, Juan in America

Ya knee-crept, Jesus-crept, swatchin' little fucker, ah'll cut the bliddy scrotum aff ye! Ah'll knacker and gut ye, ah'll eviscerate ye! Ya hure-spun, bastrified, conscrapulated young prick, ah'll do twenty years for mincin' you . . . ya parish-eyed, perishin' bastart.

Roddy MacMillan, The Bevellers (1973)

You think he's twistit. Ye want tae have seen his oul' man.

Roddy MacMillan, The Bevellers

Waldo is one of those people who would be enormously improved by death.

Saki (H.H. Munro, 1870–1916), Beasts and Super-Beasts

The wee man's gotten his parritch at last.

Observation by the Dougal Cratur on the death of Rashleigh in a dramatised version of Sir Walter Scott's Rob Roy

There ye gang, ye daft
And doitit dotterel, ye saft
Crazed outland skalrag saul.

Sydney Goodsir Smith (1915–1975), The Grace of God and the Meths Drinker

I have been the means, under God, of haanging a great number, but never just such a disjaskit rascal as yourself.

Robert Louis Stevenson (1850–1894), Weir of Hermiston

I dinna like McFarlane, I'm safe enough tae state.
His lug wad cast a shadow ower a sax-fit gate.
He's saft as ony goblin and sliddery as a skate,
McFarlane o' the Sprots o' Burnieboozie.

G. Bruce Thomson, McFarlane o' the Sprots o' Burnieboozie

He was built like a Toby-jug and his face had the complexion and texture of poisoned veal.

Jeff Torrington (1935–), The Last Shift

FOOD, DRINK AND HOSPITALITY

'Jock!' cried a farmer's wife to the cowherd, 'come awa' in
to your parritch, or the flees 'll be droonin' themsel's in
your milk bowl.'

'Nae fear o' that,' replied Jock. 'They could wade through
it.'

'Ye rogue,' she cried, 'd'ye mean to say I dinna give ye
eneuch milk?'

'Oh, aye,' said Jock, 'There's eneuch milk, for all the
parritch that's in it.'

Traditional

'It's ten years old, you know,' said the lady of the house,
pouring out some whisky for the plumber who had mended
a burst pipe.

'Aye,' he said, looking at the only part-filled glass. 'And
small for its age.'

Traditional

Our obliging landlady would, when requested, bring us a
pennyworth of soup, called *kale*, for our dinner, instead of
herring; and, if we had a little cause to remark on the want
of cleanliness in the dish, or the contents, she jocosely
replied: 'It tak's a deal o' dirt to poison sogers.'

James Anton, Retrospect of a Military Life *(1841)*

'Tell me, have you eaten that, or are you going to?'

*Sir J.M. Barrie (1860–1937), to Bernard Shaw, on looking
at Shaw's vegetarian meal. Quoted in C. Fadiman,* The
Little Brown Book of Anecdotes *(1985)*

Is there that owre his french *ragout,*
Or *olio* wad stow a sow,
Or *fricassé* wad mak her spew
Wi' perfect sconner,
Looks down wi' sneering, scornfu' view
On sic a dinner?
Poor devil! See him owre his trash,
As feckless as a wither'd rash,
His spindle shank, a guid whip-lash,
His nieve a nit:
Thro' bloody flood or field to dash,
O how unfit!

Robert Burns (1759–1796), Address to a Haggis

The cook was too filthy an object to be described; only another English gentleman whispered me and said, he believed, if the fellow was to be thrown against the wall, he would stick to it.

Edmund Burt (c. 1695–1755), Letters from a Gentleman in the North of Scotland *(1728–37), on an Edinburgh eating house*

So that's the wey o' it! Yuletide's comin'.
Haverin' hypocrites, hear them talk:
Peace and good-will to men and women,
But thraw the neck o'the bubbly-jock.

W.D. Crocker (1882–1970), The Bubbly-Jock

. . . the potato, the grossly overrated potato, that marvel of insipidity.

Norman Douglas (1868–1952), Together

For rabbits young and for rabbits old,
For rabbits hot and for rabbits cold,
For rabbits tender and for rabbits tough,
Our thanks we render – but we've had enough.

Robert Fergusson (1750–1774),
Impromptu at St Salvator's College Hall, St Andrews,
prompted by too much rabbit in the students' diet

'It's an awful thing the drink!' exclaimed a clergyman, when the barber, who was visibly affected, had drawn blood from his face for the third time.
'Aye,' replied the tonsorial artist, with a wicked leer in his eye, 'It mak's the skin tender.'

Robert Ford, Thistledown *(1901)*

Soon after his return from Scotland to London, a Scotch lady resident in the capital invited Dr Johnson to dinner, and in compliment to her distinguished guest ordered a dish of hotch-potch. When the great man had tasted it, she asked him if it was good, to which he replied with his usual gruffness, 'Very good for hogs, I believe.'
'Then, pray,' said the lady, 'let me help you to a little more.'

Robert Ford, Thistledown

After the bottle had circulated a few times, and the spirits of the assembly had begun to rise, General S–, an English trooper of fame, and a reckless *bon vivant,* arose and said, 'Gentleman, when I am in my cups, and the generous wine begins to warm my blood, I have an absurd custom of railing against the Scotch. Knowing my weakness, I hope no member of the company will take it amiss.'

He sat down, and a Highland chief, Sir Robert Bleakie, of Blair Atholl . . . quietly arose in his place, and with the utmost simplicity and good-nature, remarked, 'Gentlemen, when I am in my cups, and the generous wine begins to warm my blood, if I hear a man rail against the Scotch, I have an absurd custom of kicking him at once out of the company. Knowing my weakness, I hope no gentleman will take it amiss.'

It need scarcely be added that General S– did not on that occasion suffer himself to follow his usual custom.

Robert Ford, Thistledown, *on a London dinner party in the 1600s*

The playwright, William Douglas-Home, and his wife were invited to dinner –

'Having been to Oxford for a matinee, I duly arrived, dined, chatted and then rose to go around eleven.

"Thank you, Rachel, for a lovely dinner," said my host to my wife.

"What do you mean?" I inquired.

"I brought it over from home," Rachel explained, "as their cook was off."

"In that case," I said, "I am at liberty to say that the fish was the most disgusting thing I have ever eaten."

"That was the only dish I provided," said my host.'

From Robert Morley, A Book of Bricks

Both in a river and in a dish
I hate that ubiquitous blasted fish.

Ode to a Salmon, *recorded as having been written by 'A Commander RN, in collaboration with Flight Lieutenant James McGregor, RAF', in Arnold Silcock,* Verse and Worse *(1952)*

'That's the thing that angers me aboot an egg,' continued
the Captain. 'It never makes ye glad to see it on the table; ye
know at once the thing's a mere put-by because your wife
or Jum could not be bothered makin' something tasty.'
'We'll hae to get the hens to put their heids together and
invent a new kind o' fancy egg for sailors,' said Sunny Jim.

Neil Munro (1864–1930), The Vital Spark

The sauce-bottles are filled with old blood
above the off-white linen.

Iain Crichton Smith (1928–1998), By the Sea

'That fowl', says Brough to the landlady, 'is of a breed I
know. I knew the cut of its jib whenever it was put down.
That was the grandfather of the cock that frightened Peter.'
. . . 'Na-na, it's not so old,' says the landlady, 'but it eats
hard.'

Robert Louis Stevenson (1850–1894), Letters, *on a meal on
Iona*

A dense black substance, inimical to life.

Robert Louis Stevenson, quoted in Iain Finlayson, The
Scots *(1987), on 'black bun'*

There is great store of fowl too, as foul houses, foul sheets,
foul dishes and pots, foul trenchers and napkins . . . They
have good store of fish too, and good for those that can eat
it raw; but if it once come into their hands, it is worse than if
it were three days old: for their butter and cheese, I will not
meddle withal at this time, nor no man else at any time that
loves his life.

Sir Anthony Weldon, A Perfect Description of the People
and Country of Scotland *(1617)*

GLOSSARY OF INSULTING TERMS

bampot: idiot
bass, bassa: bastard
bauchle: worthless, shambling person
bawheid: bald-headed person
blate: shy, wimp-like
blether: chatterbox
carnaptious: argumentative
clag-tail: unwiped arse
clype: tell-tale
cuddie: donkey
dobber: idiot
dreep: feeble person
dreich: dull, grey, tedious
dreik: excrement
feartie: coward
gether-up: small, ill-dressed woman
glaikit: useless, feeble
gomeril: fool
gowk: fool (cuckoo)
haivers: nonsense, rubbish
hing-oot: dishevelled type
Irish steak: cheese
Jessie: effeminate man or boy; now obsolescent. Jessie was once one of the most popular names for a girl
keelie: a city rough, especially from Glasgow
numpty: an idiot
nyaff: a useless, no-account fellow. Usually *wee* goes in front.
nyuck: see nyaff
oof-lookin: stupid-looking
plookie: pimple-faced
radge: originally a tinkers' term for a non-tinker; now used as a general word of disparagement.

scadge: a dissolute-looking person

scunner: nuisance, annoyance, pest

shaan: no-good, hostile. A tinkers' term originally; often used with *Gadgie* (fellow). A *shaan gadgie* was someone to be distrusted.

shauchle-bodied: shaky

shilpit: feeble, shaky, sickly

snash: abusive language

sumph: great fool

teuchter: Urban and Lowland mock-Gaelic word for a Highlander: a hayseed, a bumpkin from the mountains

tumshie: idiot (literally, turnip)

wersh: insipid, tasteless; or the opposite: sharp, vinegary

GOVERNMENT

Of course us artists aren't supposed to talk about political issues, we are too idealistic, we don't have a firm enough grasp on reality . . . It's quite remarkable really the different ways whereby the state requires its artists to suck dummy tits.

James Kelman (1946–), Lecture at Glasgow School of Art, 1996

All government is a monopoly of violence.

Hugh MacDiarmid (C.M. Grieve, 1872–1978), A Glass of Pure Water

A Scandinavian-style study centre for the propagation of dullness and depression.

Robert MacNeil, The Scotsman, on Parliament, 24 February 2000

A revolving door for jobs for the boys.

Alex Salmond MSP, on Donald Dewar's first government team

Medals are given to people who've done something, and so far we've done bugger all.

Tommy Sheridan MSP, on the Scottish parliament's commemoration medals, 1999

There is no art which one government sooner learns of another than of draining money from the pockets of the people.

Adam Smith (1723–90), The Wealth of Nations

One may reasonably say that the arrangements under which Scotland was governed for a century and a quarter represented not so much a constitution as a bad joke elaborated with the careful logic of lunacy.

Colin Walkinshaw (James M. Reid), The Scots Tragedy *(1935)*

INTERNECINE INSULTS

Scotsmen ay reckon frae an ill hour.

Proverb

Sanct Petir said to God in a sport word,
'Can ye nocht mak a Helandman of this hors turd?'
God turned owre the hors turd with his pykit staff
And up start a Helandman blak as on draff.
Quod God to the Helandman, 'Quhair wilt thou now?'

'I will doun in the Lawland, Lord, and thair steill a kow.'

Anonymous, How the First Hielandman of God Was Made from Ane Hors Turd

Up wi' the souters o' Selkirk,
And down wi' the Earl o' Home.

Traditional, Up Wi' the Souters o' Selkirk

The Campbells are coming, I ken by the smell,
And when they get here we'll all send them to Hell.

Traditional, schoolboy version of The Campbells Are Comin'

'Humpback is the heir of MacLeod today, and as long as dry straw will burn, many a hump and crook there will be in the clan hereafter!'

Cried by an old woman of the Macdonalds of Eigg on a MacLeod raiding party led by Alastair Crotach (from Gaelic). The 'Eigg massacre' followed.

As long as woods have sticks,
Cummings will play foul tricks

Lochaber saw about the clan Cumming

YIRFAESISAWSKREWEDUP

Car rear window sticker seen in Glasgow, 1999

The men of Angus . . . have been growing potatoes so long that the Golden Wonder has entered into their souls.

John R. Allan, Summer in Scotland *(1938)*

Our worst enemies are our own kin in the east. They

accepted the domination of the Saxon. Got the superiority complex in so doing, and no-one looks so disdainfully now on the west-coaster as the east-coaster who has lost, or almost lost, his Gaelic . . . a pure case of the fox that lost its tail.

John Bannerman (1870–1938), Letter to his son, quoted in Bannerman: The Memoirs of Lord Bannerman of Kildonan

The two classes that mek ahl the mischief of the kintry are weemen and meenisters.

William Black (1841–1898), Highland Cousins

I am a Doric stereotype –
Abune ma brose I rift,
I skirl an birl at echtsome reels,
An darn ma hose fur thrift.

Sheena Blackhall, from Stagwyse *(1995)*

The term *Stot*, as applied to the Scotchman, was, we believe, first used in this magazine. . . In the first place a Stot is, most frequently, a sour, surly, dogged animal. He retains a most absurd resemblance to a Bull, and the absurdity is augmented by the fact that he once absolutely was a Bull . . . Look him in the face and you discern the malice of emasculation and the cowardice of his curtailed estate.

Blackwood's Magazine, *September 1822*

A poor, barren country, full of continual broils, dissensions, massacrings; a people in the last stage of rudeness and destitution . . . It is a country as yet without a soul: nothing developed in it but what is rude, external, semi-animal.

Thomas Carlyle (1795–1882), on the pre-Reformation Scots, in On Heroes and Hero-Worship

During the greater part of their history, the Scottish nation were like the conies, a feeble folk who made their houses in the rocks.

Donald Carswell, Brother Scots *(1927)*

The men o' the North are a' gone gyte,
A' gone gyte thegither, o,
The derricks rise to the Northern skies,
And the past is gane forever, o.

Sheila Douglas, The Men of the North, *quoted in Gordon Wright,* Favourite Scots Lyrics *(1973)*

Mandrag, mymmerkin, maid maister but in mows,
Thrys schield trumpir with one threid bair goun,
Say Deo mercy, or I cry the doun.

William Dunbar (c. 1460–c. 1520), to Walter Kennedy, in The Flyting of Dunbar and Kennedy

I think the Scots are a lazy set of bastards, to be quite frank . . . I don't think the work ethic is very strong.

Sir Monty Finniston (1912–), quoted in Kenneth Roy, Conversations in a Small Country *(1989)*

They are not, to put it as tactfully as possible, the most immediately lovable folk in the United Kingdom.

George Macdonald Fraser, The Steel Bonnets *(1971), on the Borderers*

The truth is we are a nation of arselickers, though we disguise it with surfaces: a surface of generous, openhanded manliness, a surface of dour practical integrity, a surface of futile maudlin defiance like when we break goalposts and windows after football matches on foreign soil and commit suicide on Hogmanay by leaping from fountains in Trafalgar Square.

Alasdair Gray (1934–), 1982 Janine

. . . we should be cautious when we assume we are unique. Other people may be just as crazy as we are.

Cliff Hanley (1922–99), 'A State of Mind', from The Sunday Mail Story of Scotland *(1988)*

Presumably because of nationalist successes at the polls, men I thought had slunk away to prickly sulks on couches of thistles or even to realise in which decade of which century they lived in, came breengin' hurriedly back, reknitting their half-unravelled claymores, and pulling behind them pramfuls of young poets waving tartan rattles.

Alan Jackson (1938–), 'The Knitted Claymore', in Lines Review *(June 1971)*

As for the Highlands, I shortly comprehend them all in two sorts of people: the one, that dwelleth in our mainland, that are barbarous for the most part, and yet mixed with some show of civility: the other that dwelleth in the Isles, and are utterly barbarous.

King James VI (1566–1625), Basilikon Doron

Our gentyl men are all degenerate;
Liberalitie and Lawtie, both are lost;
And cowardice with lordis is laureate;
And knichtlie courage turnit in brag and boast.

Sir David Lindsay (c. 1490–1555), The Complaint of the Commoun Weill of Scotland

... swordless Scotland, sadder than its psalms,
Fosters its sober youth on national alms
To breed a dull provincial discipline,
Commerce its god, and golf its anodyne.

Eric Linklater (1899–1974), quoted in Hugh MacDiarmid,
Lucky Poet *(1943)*

... they contracted ideas and habits, quite incompatible
with the customs of regular society and civilized life,
adding greatly to those defects which characterize persons
living in a loose and unreformed state of society.

James Loch (1780–1855), architect of the Sutherland
clearances, giving his views on the inhabitants of Sutherland,
quoted in Ian Grimble, The Trial of Patrick Sellar *(1962)*

Scotland's Image? You must be joking!
The less said about that the better . . .
Scotland's image? The hell with it!
I love, I curse, I hate, I care
that we alone should dare submit
we are to *what we think we were!*

Tyrell McConall (1941–), quoted in M. Lindsay, Scotland:
An Anthology *(1974)*

Nearly all the prominent people in Scottish public life today
. . . remind me of the oxpeckers, an African genus of
starlings. These birds are parasitic on the large mammals
whose bodies they search for ticks and other vermin . . . So
strikingly prehensile are their claws that Millais relates that
when 'a dead bird that had grown stiff was thrown on the
back and sides of an ox, so that the feet touched the
animal's hide, the claws held fast at once, and could not
easily be withdrawn'. That is precisely the relationship of

most of these people (all dead – born dead, in fact) to
Scottish life.

Hugh MacDiarmid (C.M. Grieve, 1892–1978), Lucky Poet

You remember the place called the Tawny Field?
It got a fine dose of manure;
Not the dung of sheep and goats
But Campbell blood, well congealed.

Iain Lom Macdonald (c. 1620–c. 1707), Las Inbhir
Lochaidh (The Battle of Inverlochy), *translated by Derick
Thomson*

The Scottish Celts . . . like all peoples preponderantly
peasant in outlook, they worship money and titles.

Alasdair Alpin MacGregor, The Western Isles *(1949)*

. . . morals, in the sexual sense, are extremely lax in the
Western Isles . . . Bastardy has long been common – nay
notorious – in the Highlands and Islands.

Alasdair Alpin MacGregor, The Western Isles

A jocular anecdote of old blind Mr Stewart (of Appin). The
boy who was reading to him from the Book of Job
mispronounced the word *camels.* – 'If he had so many
Cawmells in his household,' said Mr Stewart, 'I do not
wonder at his misthriving.'

Henry Mackenzie (1745–1831), The Anecdotes and
Egotisms of Henry Mackenzie, *a dig at Clan Campbell*

Lowland Scots and Covenanters
Do the same as Stewart kings:
Give them a London title,

And their back's to Edinburgh.

Donald MacIntyre (1889–1964), When the Stone Was Returned *(from Gaelic)*

Alasdair. . . if grace goes with gloom, great is the good you have got from God.

Donnchadh Mac an Phearsùinn, from a poem in the Book of the Dean of Lismore, *early 16th century (from Gaelic)*

No other country has fallen so hard for its own image in the funfair mirror. Tartan rock, and a Scottie dog for every pot.

Candia MacWilliam (1957–), A Case of Knives

Of Liddisdale the common thievis
Sa pertlie stealis now and reivis,
That nane may keep
Horse, nolt, nor sheep,
Nor yet dar sleep for their mischiefis.

Sir Richard Maitland (1496–1586), Aganis the Thievis of Liddisdale

Polwart, ye peip like a mouse among thornes,
No cunning ye keip; Polwart, ye peip,
Ye luik lyk a sheip and ye had twa hornes.

Alexander Montgomerie (c. 1545–1611), The Flyting of Montgomerie and Patrick Hume of Polwarth

Scottish streets are given an atmosphere of their own simply by the number of drunk people that one encounters in them.

Edwin Muir (1887–1959), Scottish Journey *(1935)*

Bewar what thou speikes, little foull earthe taid,

With thy Canigait breeks, bewar what thou speiks,
Or ther sall be weit cheikes for the last that thou made ...
And we mell thou sall yet, little cultron cuist.

Alexander Montgomerie, The Flyting of Montgomerie and
Polwarth

Kaily lippis, kis my hippis, in grippis thou's behint ...
Jock Blunt, thrawin frunt, kis the cunt of ane kow

Patrick Hume of Polwarth, The Flyting of Montgomerie
and Polwarth

If Freud had known anything about Scotland he would have
left Vienna like an arrow and taken on the whole population
as a collective patient, to treat the national neurosis, the
compulsive obsessive rigidity that permeates the population.

Alastair Reid, Whereabouts *(1987)*

... that plateau of uncomfortable, grunt-punctuated
silence which Borderers seem to inhabit most of the time.

Alastair Reid, Borderlines, *in K. Miller,* Memoirs of a
Modern Scotland *(1971)*

Oh, that's Scotland. All the families are odd, very odd.

William Soutar (1898–1943), Symposium

... a Stewart, nae doubt – they all hing together like bats in
a steeple.

Robert Louis Stevenson (1850–1894), Kidnapped

Ah don't hate the English. They're just wankers. We're
colonised by wankers ... We're ruled by effete arseholes.
What does that make us? The lowest of the fuckin

low . . . the most wretched, servile, miserable pathetic trash that was ever shat intae creation. Ah don't hate the English. They just git oan wi the shite thuv goat. Ah hate the Scots.

Irvine Welsh (1957–), Trainspotting

JIBES AND PUT-DOWNS

Traditional

Awa' an' bile yer heid.

Awa' and raffle yer onions.

Away to Banff and gether buckies.

Aebody's queer but you an' me: an' sometimes *you're* queer.

Does your mither ken you're oot?

He's yin o' thae etten-an'-spewed characters.

He thinks he's honey but the bees don't know.

If I had a belly like yours I'd tie it to a tree and let the birds peck it.

If she was chocolate she wad eat hersel.

My wee wife's a bonny wee wife:
Your wee wife's a deevil.

She has a face like a burst couch.

Shut your legs – here's a car comin'.

Skinny malinky lang-legs, big banana feet,
Went tae the pictures and couldna find a seat.

Tak' a long walk affa short pier.

Ye'll be a man before your mither.

Yer tongue wad clip cloots.

Ye've got a face like a melted welly.

From J. T. R. Ritchie, The Singing Street *(1964), and other sources*

JUDGEMENTS OF VARIOUS KINDS

On Accents

The accent of the lowest state of Glaswegians is the ugliest one can encounter . . . it is associated with the unwashed and the violent.

Anonymous university lecturer (1975), quoted in Janet Menzies, Investigation of Attitudes to Scots and Glaswegian Dialect Among Secondary School Pupils

Good God! I hope not. I would rather the country was sunk in the sea. *I*, the Scotch accent!

Lord Byron (1788–1824), when told he had a slight Scots accent, quoted in E.C. Mayne, Byron *(1924)*

If an announcer pronounces 'Boer War' with the accent of Barra or the accent of Buchan, fair enough, but if he pronounces 'Boer War' as if he were a Pekingese barking defiance (*baw waw! baw waw!*) he should be out on his neck.

Hamish Henderson (1920–2002), letter to The Scotsman, *9 February 1953*

You could drive a train across the Firth of Forth on her vowels.

Bruce Marshall (1899–1987), Teacup Terrace

On Africa

I take it Africa was brought about in sheer ill humour. No one can think it possible that an all-wise God (had he been in his sober senses) would create a land and fill it full of people destined to be replaced by other people from across the seas.

R.B. Cunninghame Graham (1852–1936), 'Bloody Niggers', *from* Selected Writings, *edited by Cedric Watt (1981)*

On the Albert Monument, London

. . . a monument whereat the nations stand aghast.

Norman Douglas (1868–1952)

On Americans

Aye, they have a great population, viz. 21 millions of the greatest bores that the moon ever saw.
David Livingstone (1813–73), letter to his parents, 26 September 1852

On the Animal Kingdom
Whae's like us? -
Damned few,
an'
we're
aw
deid.

Douglas Lipton (1953–), Great Auk

On a BBC Announcer

At least he shall never read the Epilogue.

*Lord Reith (1889–1971), head of the BBC, when persuaded
not to sack an announcer who had been divorced, quoted in
Ned Sherrin,* Theatrical Anecdotes *(1991)*

On Booksellers

. . . if you would knock any brains into a bookseller you
would have my consent, but not to knock out any part of the
portion with which Heaven has endowed them.

Sir Walter Scott (1771–1832), letter to James Hogg, 1820

On Boys

'You're like every other boy that was born, picked up from
the Bass Rock you were, that's where your father got you,
didn't you know? Why didn't he go to the May Island, the
silly kipper that he was, and bring us back a nice wee lassie
instead of you, you nasty little brat.'

Christopher Rush, A Twelvemonth and a Day *(1985)*

All my life I have loved a womanly woman and admired a

manly man, but I never could stand a boily boy.

Lord Rosebery (1847–1929)

On the Burns Cult

We went to the Cottage, and took some whisky . . . Oh, the flummery of a birth-place. Cant! cant! cant! It is enough to give a spirit the guts-ache.

John Keats (1795–1821), Letters, on a visit to Burns's birthplace

On Businessmen

People of the same trade seldom meet together even for merriment and diversion but the conversation ends in a conspiracy against the public, or in some contrivance to raise prices.

Adam Smith (1723–90), The Wealth of Nations

On a Caithnessian

He seems a fine enough loon but ye can never tell with a Gallagh. Ye canna understand what they say half the time.

George Gunn, The Gold of Kildonan (1989)

On Children

I abominate the sight of them so much that I have always had the greatest respect for the character of Herod.

Lord Byron (1788–1824), letter to Augusta Leigh, 30 August 1811

On the Common People

Who o'er the herd would wish to reign,
Fantastic, fickle, fierce, and vain?
 . . . Thou many-headed monster-thing,
O who would wish to be thy king?

Sir Walter Scott (1771–1832), The Lady of the Lake

On Conscription

Fat civilians wishing they
'Could go and fight the Hun.'
Can't you see them thanking God
That they're over forty-one?

E. A. Mackintosh (1893–1916), Recruiting

On Critics

One good critic could demolish all this *dreck,* but one good
critic is precisely what we do not have. Instead we are
lumbered with pin-money pundits, walled-up academics or
old ladies of both sexes.

*Eddie Boyd (1916–1989), on Scottish drama and drama
critics, in* Cencrastus *(Autumn 1987)*

A coward brood, which mangle as they prey,
By hellish instinct, all that cross their way;
Aged or young, the living or the dead
No mercy find – these harpies must be fed.

Lord Byron (1788–1824), English Bards and Scotch Reviewers

Every critic in the town
Runs the minor poet down;
Every critic – don't you know it?

Is himself a minor poet.

R.F. Murray (1863–1894)

On Darwinism

I have no patience whatever with these gorilla
damnifications of humanity.

Thomas Carlyle (1795–1881), on Charles Darwin's The
Origin of Species

On a Fallen Woman

Near some lamp-post, wi' dowy face,
Wi' heavy een, and sour grimace,
Stands she that beauty lang had kend,
Whoredom her trade, and vice her end.

Robert Fergusson (1750–1774), Auld Reekie

On Films

Braveheart is pure Australian shite. Unless William
Wallace went about with Dulux on his fuckin' face, in
pigtails and a kilt. And then there's Rob Roy, poncing about
the heather talking about honour. He was a spy, a thief, a
blackmailer – a cunt, basically.

Billy Connolly (1942–), interview with Bob Flynn in The
Guardian, *April 1996*

On the Folk Tradition

. . . the boring doggerel of analphabetic and ineducable
farm-labourers, tinkers and the like.

Hugh MacDiarmid (C.M. Grieve, 1892–1978), letter to The Scotsman, *9 January 1960*

On Fortune

Ne'er mind how Fortune waft and warp;
She's but a bitch.

Robert Burns (1759–1796), Second Epistle to J. Lapraik

On the Future

The future is not what it used to be.

Sir Malcolm Rifkind, in Talking Politics, *BBC Radio, 1988*

On Gay Men

We don't get God saying, 'Poor little gay men, we'll have to open the church hall and let them have their own little gay church and their own gay minister.'
God says, 'To death with them.'

Pastor Jack Glass, quoted in Steve Bruce, No Pope of Rome *(1985)*

On Glasgow's New Water Supply

I just canna thole that new water: it's got neither taste nor smell.

Old Glaswegian lady, quoted in Elizabeth Haldane, The Scotland of Our Fathers *(1933)*

On Grouse Shooters

The grouse shooters were often rather pathetic people,

going through a ritual imposed on them because they could afford it . . . They were stung, by everything and by everybody.

John R. Allan, Farmer's Boy

On Halitosis

His breath's like a burst lavy, ye could strip paint wi' it.

Tony Roper, The Steamie *(1987)*

On Handwriting

The dawn of legibility in his handwriting has revealed his utter inability to spell.

Attributed to Ian Hay (John Hay Beith, 1876–1952)

On the Hebrideans

. . . many an Islander is seldom fully awake much before noon! If the pubs be open then or shortly afterwards, it is doubtful whether, on certain days, he is ever entirely in full possession of his faculties. Drink certainly exaggerates his temperamental laziness.

Alasdair Alpin MacGregor, The Western Isles *(1949)*

On Highlanders

'Now,' Bonnie Prince Charlie is reputed to have said, on first donning the kilt, 'now I should be a complete Highlander, if only I had the itch.'

G.S. Fraser (1915–1980), Scotland

On Historians

If you should bid me count the lies of Hector's History, I might as well assay to sum the stars or waves of the sea,

John Leland on Hector Boece's Scotorum Historiae, *published in 1527*

Scottish historiography has been for too long bogged down in a preoccupation with the myriad aspects of the Labour movement and associated areas of working-class history, to the exclusion of wider themes left virtually untouched. Short of an actual census of head lice among the children of handloom weavers in the nineteenth century, no detail of proletarian experience has been left unexplored.

Gerald Warner, The Scottish Tory Party *(1988)*

On Hogmanay

Dolly: That's whit ah like aboot this time o' the year, ye meet people ye've never met before.
Magrit: Aye . . . an usually ye hope ye'll never meet them again.

Tony Roper, The Steamie *(1987)*

On Humanitarians

They are all alike, these humanitarian lovers of first causes. Always ready to burn something, or somebody; always ready with their cheerful Hell-fire and gnashing of teeth.

Norman Douglas (1868–1952), Old Calabria

On Incest (and Folk-dancing)

You should make a point of trying every experience once,

except incest and folk-dancing.

'Anonymous Scotsman' quoted by Sir Arnold Bax (1883–1953) in Farewell My Youth *(1943)*

On Industrial Improvement

We cam na here to view your warks,
In hopes to be mair wise,
But only, lest we gang to hell,
It may be no surprise.

Robert Burns (1759–1796), Impromptu on Carron Ironworks

And call they this Improvement? – to have changed,
My native Clyde, thy once romantic shore,
Where nature's face is banished and estranged,
And Heaven reflected in thy wave no more;
Whose banks, that sweetened May-day's breath before,
Lie sere and leafless now in summer's beam,
With sooty exhalations covered o'er;
And for the daisied green sward, down thy stream
Unsightly brick-lanes smoke, and clanking engines
gleam.

Thomas Campbell (1777–1844), Lines on Revisiting a Scottish River

On the Inhabitants of Inverness

If justice were down to the inhabitants of Inverness, in twenty years' time there would be no-one left there but the Provost and the hang-man.

John Telford (d. 1807), quoted in L.T.C. Rolt, Thomas Telford *(1958)*

On Inventing

Of all things in life there is nothing more foolish than inventing.

James Watt (1736–1819), quoted in H.W. Dickinson, James Watt *(1936)*

On Jurymen

Argyleshire stots make the stupidest jurymen.

Lord Cockburn (1779–1854), Circuit Journeys

On William MacGonagall

William MacGonagall was not a bad poet; still less a good bad poet. He was not a poet at all.

Hugh MacDiarmid (C.M. Grieve, 1892–1978), Scottish Eccentrics

On Metaphysics

The science appeared to me an elaborate, diabolical invention for mystifying what was clear, and confounding what was intelligible.

W.E. Aytoun (1813–1865)

On Millionaires

A millionaire's just a shameless thief

Mary Brooksbank (1897–1980), 'To the Erudite', from Sidlaw Breezes

On Mons Meg

. . . a monument of our pride and poverty. The size is immense, but six smaller guns would have been made at the same expense, and done six times as much execution as she could have done.

Sir Walter Scott (1771–1832), Journals

On Mothers-in-Law

Wi' every effort to be fair
And no undue antagonism
I canna but say that my sweetheart's mither
Is a moolie besom, a moolie besom,
Naething but a moolie besom!

Hugh MacDiarmid (1892–1978), A Moolie Besom

On the Name Grizel

. . . for some strange reason I can never hear it pronounced without thinking of a Polar bear eating an Eskimo.

Lewis Grassic Gibbon (James Leslie Mitchell, 1901–35),
Scottish Scene

On Niagara Falls

Naething but a perfect waste o' watter.
Anonymous citizen of Paisley

On Nicknames

. . . the most interesting nicknames . . . were those descriptive and often highly offensive appellations referring to personal appearance, habits and behaviour. Thus we find Curst Eckie, Ill Will Armstrong, Nebless Clem Croser, the two Elliott brothers, Archie and George, who were familiarly known as 'Dog Pyntle' and 'Buggerback'.

George Macdonald Fraser, The Steel Bonnets *(1971)*

On Officers

. . . at school that symbol o' extermination was called Fozie Tam

James Hogg (1770–1835), quoted in Christopher North (John Wilson, 1785–1854), Noctes Ambrosianae

The captain's all right, really. A touch of the toasted tea-breid. You know the type.

W. Gordon Smith, Mr Jock *(1987)*

On Oil-Men

Hammered like a bolt
diagonally through Scotland (my
small dark country) this
train's a
swaying caveful of half–
seas over oilmen (fuck
this fuck that fuck
everything) bound for Aberdeen and
North Sea Crude

Liz Lochhead (1947–), Inter-City

On Orangeism

. . . one of the least edifying brands of virulent religious
fanaticism. Orangeism is alien to the Scottish tradition. Its
mythology is a farrago of unhistorical balderdash.

Hamish Henderson (1920–2002), letter to the Edinburgh
Evening Dispatch, *7 July 1951*

On Poets

. . . men wha through the ages sit,
And never move frae aff the bit,
Wha hear a Burns or Shakespeare sing,
Yet still their ain bit jingles string,
As they were worth the fashioning

Hugh MacDiarmid (C.M. Grieve, 1892–1978), A Drunk
Man Looks at the Thistle

Ne'er
Was flattery lost on poet's ear;
A simple race! they waste their toil
For the vain tribute of a smile.

Sir Walter Scott (1771–1832), The Lay of the Last Minstrel

On Political Economy

. . . what we might call, by way of eminence, *the dismal
science.*

Thomas Carlyle (1795–1881), The Nigger Question

On an Over-Proud Man

Too coy to flatter, and too proud to serve,

Thine be the joyless dignity to starve.

Tobias Smollett (1721–1771), Advice

On the Press

. . . journalism suits the Scots as it is a profession into which you can crawl without enquiry as to your qualifications, and because it is a profession in which the most middling talents will take you a long way.

T.W. Crosland, The Unspeakable Scot *(1902)*

I have long ago learnt that the only true things in the newspapers are the advertisements.

Norman Lamont, quoted in The Independent, *3 December 1994*

. . . to me the press is the mouth of a sewer, where lying is professed as from a university chair, and everything prurient, and ignoble, and essentially dull finds its abode and pulpit.

Robert Louis Stevenson (1850–1894), letter to Edmund Gosse

bitch journalism

Sir David Steel, President of the Scottish Parliament, September 1999

On the Public

I do not like mankind; but men, and not all of these – and fewer women. As for respecting the race, and, above all, that fatuous rabble of burgesses called 'the public', God save me from such irreligion!

Robert Louis Stevenson (1850–1894), letter to Edmund Gosse

On Publishers

They say that when the author was on the scaffold he said goodbye to the ministers and reporters, and then he saw some publishers sitting in the front row below, and to them he did not say goodbye. He said instead, 'I'll see you later.'

Sir J.M. Barrie, Speech to the Aldine Club, New York (1896)

Napoleon is a tyrant, a monster, the sworn foe of our nation. But gentlemen – he once shot a publisher.

Thomas Campbell (1777–1844), proposing a toast to Napoleon Bonaparte at a writers' dinner

It is with publishers as with wives: one always wants someone else's.

Norman Douglas (1868–1952)

On the Reformation

The Reformation was a kind of spiritual strychnine of which Scotland took an overdose.

Willa Muir (1890–1970), Mrs Grundy in Scotland

On Respectability

The Scot . . . makes a great parade of his respectability and takes a genuine pride in it, just as a savage takes a great

pride in his store clothes; but there is always the secret
hankering for the loin-cloth and feathers, and sometimes it
has its way.

Donald Carswell, Brother Scots *(1927)*

On Rozie o' the Cleugh

I'll gie thee Rozie o' the Cleugh,
I'm sure she'll please thee weel eneuch.
Up wi' her on the bare bane dyke:
She'll be rotten or I'll be ripe.

Anonymous, Hey, Wully Wine

On the Scott Monument

I am sorry to report the Scott Monument a failure. It is like
the spire of a Gothic church taken off and stuck in the ground.

Charles Dickens (1812–1870)

The wise people of Edinburgh built . . . a small vulgar Gothic
steeple on the ground and called it the Scott Monument.

John Ruskin (1819–1900)

On Scottish Nationalism

Let's be glad that one king and one bloody frontier have
gone and recognise that the world has suffered enough from
men surrendering their freedoms to ideologies, nation-
states, religions and football-clubs.

Alan Jackson (1938–), 'The Knitted Claymore' in Lines
Review, *June 1971*

On a Show-off

He doesnae juist drap a name
or set it up and say grace wi't,
he lays it oot upon his haun
and hits ye richt in the face wi't.
T.S. Law (1916–), Importance

On Slugs

Snails too lazy to build a shed.

George Macdonald (1824–1905), Little Boy Blue

On Smoking

 . . . Is it not both great vanitie and uncleanness, that at the
table, a place of respect, of cleanlinesse, of modestie, men
should not be ashamed, to sit tossing of Tobacco pipes, and
puffing of the smoke of Tobacco one to another, making the
filthy smoke and stink thereof, to exhale athwart the dishes,
and infect the aire, when very often men that abhorre it are
at their repast?

King James VI (1566–1625), A Counterblaste to Tobacco

On taxi-drivers

The stamp-peyin self-employed ur truly the lowest form ay
vermin oan god's earth.

Irvine Welsh (1957–), Trainspotting

On Television in Scotland

You just have to watch the Scottish BAFTAs to want to kill
yourself.

Muriel Gray (1959–), interview in Scotland on Sunday, *14
January 1996*

On Thiggers

Some little of the thiggers' styles I will set forth; they are
Roving-eye sons, Fly-by-night sons while yet far off.
They are Early-rising sons, who on a summer's day demand
    more sun; Spyer-sons,
Greedy-sons are they all.

*Giolla Coluim MacMhuirich (15th century), from a poem
on thiggers (abusers of hospitality) in the* Book of the Dean
of Lismore *(from Gaelic)*

On the Unco-Guid

O ye wha are sae guid yoursel,
Sae pious and sae holy,
Ye've nought to do but mark and tell
Your neibours' fauts and folly!

Robert Burns (1759–1796), Address to the Unco Guid, or
the Rigidly Righteous

On the Un-reasoning

He who will not reason is a bigot; he who cannot is a fool;
and he who dares not, is a slave.

William Drummond (1585–1649), Academical Question

On Up-rooters of Trees

Primitive people used to worship trees . . . if their beliefs
have any foundation in truth I know some Fife farmers who
must go haunted to their graves.

Christopher Rush, A Twelvemonth and a Day *(1985)*

On Warfare

Ye hypocrites! are these your pranks?
To murder men, and gie God thanks!
For shame! Gie o'er – proceed no farther –
God won't accept your thanks for murther.

Robert Burns (1759–1796), Verses Written on a Pane of
Glass on the Occasion of a National Thanksgiving for a
Naval Victory

On Women MPs

The women in the House of Commons are mostly hideous.
They have no fragrance . . . cagmags, scrubheaps, old tattles.

Sir Nicholas Fairbairn (1933–1995), obituary in The
Scotsman, *February 1995, quoted in A. Cran and J.
Robertson,* Dictionary of Scottish Quotations *(1996)*

On Youth

There is a great deal more to be said about youth, but very
little in its favour. Its most attractive qualities – its only
attractive qualities – are innocence and physical beauty. But
these are not in themselves sources of illimitable interest.

James Bridie (Osborne Henry Mavor, 1888–1957), Mr
Bridie's Alphabet for little Glasgow highbrows

THE KIRK, GOD AND THE DEVIL

There is more knavery among kirkmen than honesty among courtiers.

Anonymous

An old tale from the west relates that St Columba and St Moluag were engaged in a race to be first to reach the isle of Lismore and convert its inhabitants to Christianity. Seeing Columba gaining, Moluag chopped off his little finger and threw it to land, thus claiming possession. Irked, Columba cried:

'May you have the alder for your firewood.'

'The Lord will make the alder burn pleasantly,' replied Moluag.

'May you have the jagged ridges for your pathway,' said Columba.

'The Lord will smooth them to the feet,' replied Moluag.

St Andreus is an Atheist, and Glasgow is ane gouke:
A wencher Brechin: Edinburgh of avarice a pocke:
To popery prone is Galloway: Dunkeld is rich in thesaure . . .
O quhat a shame Christ's flock to trust to such unfaithful
    dogs

Anonymous pasquil on the Scottish Bishops, from the 1630s

An elderly Highlander, who had grown tired of the internecine squabbles and schisms of the small Presbyterian sect to which he had long belonged, confided to a friend: 'Sometimes I think I'll just give up religion altogether; and start going to the Church of Scotland.'

Traditional

A parish minister was reproving one of his parishioners for his frequent failures to come to the church service. The man muttered something about the services being 'too long', which annoyed the minister even more.

'One day, you know, you'll end up in a place where there are no sermons, either long or short,' he said.

'Aye, and maybe it won't be for a lack of ministers,' said the other.

Traditional

Thou knowest that the silly snivelling body is not worthy even to keep a door in thy house. Cut him down as a cumberer of the ground; tear him up root and branch, and cast the wild rotten stump out of the vineyard. Thresh him, o Lord, and dinna spare! O thresh him tightly with the flail of thy wrath, and mak a strae wisp of him to stap the mouth o' Hell.

Anonymous Seceder minister, preaching on the green at Symington, against the parish minister, quoted in Agnes Mure Mackenzie, Scottish Pageant 1707–1802 *(1950)*

Pisky, Pisky, Amen,
Down on your knees and up again.

Rude boys' chant to Episcopalians, quoted in H. Grey Graham, The Social Life of Scotland in the Eighteenth Century *(1899)*

'We thank thee, O Lord, for all thy mercies; such as they are.'

Anonymous Aberdeen minister, quoted in William Power, Scotland and the Scots *(1934)*

One is tempted almost to say that there was more of Jesus in St Theresa's little finger than in John Knox's whole body.

Matthew Arnold (1822–1888), Literature and Dogma

My father had a strong dislike for marriages of necessity, common enough at one time in Scotland.He was called to officiate at one of these, and arrived with reluctance and disgust half an hour late. 'You are very late, Mr Baird,' said the bridegroom. 'Yes, about six months too late,' replied Mr Baird.

John Logie Baird (1888–1946), on his father, in Sermons, Soap and Television

Let us exorcise
the old god of Scotland
with his knotted brain and jellyfish eyes
who has tormented his children
from generation unto generation.

Tom Buchan (1931–1995), Exorcism

When the Scotch Kirk was at the height of its power, we may search history in vain for any institution which can compete with it, except the Spanish Inquisition.

Henry Thomas Buckle (1821–1862), History of Civilisation in England

As cauld a wind as ever blew,
A caulder kirk, and in't but few;
As cauld a preacher's ever spak'
Ye'll a' be het ere I come back.

Robert Burns (1759–1796), On a Church Service at Lamington

An' now, auld 'Cloots', I ken ye're thinkin,
A certain bardie's rantin, drinkin,
Some luckless hour will send him linkin'
To your black pit;
But, faith! he'll turn a corner jinkin,
An' cheat you yet.

Robert Burns, Address to the Deil

There is one place in the Universe where God and the Devil join hands. That place is Scotland.

H. J. Cameron (1873–c. 1930)

Begg belonged to the old native stock, the surliest, crassest and most fanatical in Scotland. He was typical of the breed, a man of mean intellect and little culture . . . a truculent and vindictive bully whose influence in the councils of the Church was won and maintained by a system of terrorism and coarse intrigue.

Donald Carswell, Brother Scots *(1927), on the Rev. James Begg, minister of Newington Free Church*

'Mr ——, you must cut out one half of that sermon. It doesn't matter which half.'

Dr Thomas Chalmers (1780–1847) to an Edinburgh divinity student, quoted in William Knight, Some Nineteenth-Century Scotsmen *(1903)*

King James VI was complaining of the leanness of his hunting horse, when his fool, Archy Armstrong, said he could tell how to make the horse fatter in a very short time. 'How is that?' said the king.
'Make him a bishop,' replied Archy, 'and if he is not soon as fat as he can wallow, then ride me!'

From Robert Chambers, Scottish Jests and Anecdotes *(1832)*

. . . not a religion for gentlemen.

King Charles II (1630–1685), persuading his minister, Lauderdale, to give up Presbyterianism for Episcopacy

Then the folk were sair pitten aboot,
An' they cried, as the weather grew waur:
'Oh Lord! We ken we hae sinn'd,
But a joke can be carried owre far!'
Then they chapped at the ark's muckle door,
To speir gin douce Noah had room;
But Noah never heedit their cries;
He said, 'This'll learn ye to soom.'

W.D. Cocker (1882–1970), The Deluge

The minister (and Moderator of the Kirk) David Williamson, who lived in the latter part of the 17th century and the early 18th, enjoyed a special notoriety by having married no less than seven wives in succession. His contemporaries speculated freely on the reasons for his sexual prowess, the most popular suggestion being that he possessed three testicles:

. . . he made numerous converts, and its odd
Not more by preaching than his ponderous codd,
Or stone, that had of weight and vigour more
Than the other two he carried straight befor;
The cause he finger'd them oft was not his choice,
But force to keep them in an equal poise. . .
After three score he married the seventh wife.
And to his dying day could mount his pole,
And like any old rat penetrat each hole.
Mr Finnie, Elegy on the Death of Williamson, *from James Maidment,* Scottish Pasquils *(1868)*

. . . a base impudent brazen-faced villain, a spiteful ignorant pedant, a gross idolator, a mere slanderer, an evil man, hardened against all shame . . . full of insolence and abuse, chicanery and nonsense, detestable, misty, erroneous, wicked, vile, pernicious, terrible and horrid doctrines, tending to corrupt the mind and stupify the conscience, with gross iniquity, audacious hostility, pitiful evasion, base, palpable and shocking deceit

The Rev Adam Gib (fl. 17th century), anti-Burgher leader, reviewing a work by the Rev Archibald Hill, a Burgher minister, from a pamphlet printed in Perth (1782)

'Religion – a Scot know religion? Half of them think of God as a Scot with brosy morals and a penchant for Burns. And the other half are over damned mean to allow the Almighty even existence.'

Lewis Grassic Gibbon (James Leslie Mitchell, 1901–1935), Cloud Howe

Three generations of one family were ministers – two of them university professors of divinity. The general view was that talent had declined in each stage. Someone mentioned to the Rev. Dr Gillan, of Paisley, that he had heard the grandson preach.
'What kind of a sermon was it?' asked Gillan. 'If it had both manner and matter, it would be the grandfaither's; if it had matter, but no manner, it would be the faither's; and if it had neither matter nor manner, it would be his ain.'

From John Gillespie, Humours of Scottish Life, *1904*

Two rude boys in Dumfries shouted to to the minister, the Rev Walter Dunlop,
'Hey, maister! The de'ils deid!'

To which he replied, 'In that case I must pray for two fatherless bairns.'

Recorded in Alexander Hislop, The Book of Scottish Anecdote *(1883)*

'I hope you are pleased with my preaching this afternoon, John,' said a vain young probationer to the beadle who was disrobing him in the vestry after the sermon.
'It was *all sound,* sir,' said John, with a sly expression.

Alexander Hislop, The Book of Scottish Anecdote

. . . upon the whole, we may conclude, that the *Christian Religion* not only was at first attended by miracles, but even at this day cannot be believed by any reasonable person without one.

David Hume (1711–1776), An Essay Concerning Human Understanding

In all ages of the world, priests have been enemies of liberty.

David Hume, Of the Parties of Great Britain

What is betwixt the pride of a glorious Nebuch-adnezzar and the preposterous humility of our puritan ministers, claiming to their parity, and crying, 'We are all but vile worms'; and yet wil judge and give law to their king, but will be judged nor controlled by none. Surely there is more pride under such a one's black bonnet than under great Alexander's diadem.

King James VI (1566–1625), Basilikon Doron

The High Church . . . high only in the sense that game is high – when it is decomposing.

Attributed to Lord Kelvin (1824–1907) in Angela Cran and James Robertson, Dictionary of Scottish Quotations *(1996)*

I think Calvinism has done more harm to Scotland than drugs ever did.

R.D. Laing (1927–89), speaking in Iona Abbey, 1984

. . . the minister's voice
spread a pollution of bad beliefs.

Norman MacCaig (1910–96), Highland Funeral

Religion? Huh!

Hugh MacDiarmid (C.M. Grieve, 1892–1978), Two Memories

I saw twa items on
The TV programme yesterday.
'General Assembly of the Church of Scotland'
Said ane – the ither 'Nuts in May'.
I lookit at the picters syne
But which was which I couldna say.

Hugh MacDiarmid, Nuts in May

As far as I'm concerned, Scotland will be reborn when the last minister is strangled with the last copy of the *Sunday Post*.

Tom Nairn (1932–), The Three Dreams of Scottish Nationalism, *in Karl Miller,* Memoirs of a Modern Scotland *(1970)*

I cannot praise the Doctor's eyes,
I never saw his glance divine;
He always shuts them when he prays,
And when he preaches I shut mine.

George Outram (1806–1850), recorded in Alexander Hislop, The Book of Scottish Anecdote *(1883)*

I've read the secret name o' Knox's God,
The gowd calf 'Getting On'.

Tom Scott (1918–), Fergus

O ay! the Monks! the Monks! they did the mischief!
Theirs all the grossness, all the superstition,
Of a most gross and superstitious age.

Sir Walter Scott (1771–1832), The Monastery

What has the Kirk given us? Ugly churches and services,
identifying in the minds of the churchgoers ugliness with
God, have stifled the Scottish arts almost out of existence
. . . Until the Kirk as it has been is dead Scotland will
continue to be the Home of Lost Causes.

George Scott-Moncrieff (1910–), in D.C. Thomson, Scotland
in Quest of Her Youth: A Scrutiny *(1932)*

Coatbridge youth Sean O'Brien (16) died recently whilst
doing a Y. O. P. course at a factory. Sean (a good British
name) went to dry himself at a heater unaware that his
boiler suit was soaked in paraffin . . . Sean's father Dennis
said it was a pity this had happened as Sean was just
warming to the job . . . Sean disproved the old theory that
Shite does not burn.

Scottish Loyalist View, *1983–84, quoted in Steve Bruce,*
No Pope of Rome *(1985)*

Covenanters. Hopeless cases committed to hopeless causes.
Ten thousand martyrs, but no saints.

W. Gordon Smith, Mr Jock *(1987)*

A feckless crew, no worth a preen,
As bad as Smith o' Aiberdeen.

Robert Louis Stevenson (1850–1894), on the Rev. W. Robertson Smith, tried for heresy by the Free Church

I assert without fear of contradiction, that if they had never known it, and some missionary brought home an account of its marvels as belonging to the faith of some Polynesian islanders, they would be filled with wonder and compassion at the monstrous superstition of these poor heathen barbarians.

James Thomson ('B.V.', 1834–1882), Cope's Tobacco Plant, *on those who accept the Book of Revelation as Holy Writ*

. . . a supernatural religion, whose roots cling deep in the past, whose branches and scions extend over all regions of the earth, whose evil shadow chills and darkens our richest fields of culture and civilisation.

James Thomson, on Christianity, in the National Reformer

The Bischop wald nocht wed ane wyfe,
The Abbot not persew ane,
Thinkand it was ane lustie lyfe,
Ilk day to haif a new ane.

The Brothers Wedderburn, The Paip, That Pagane Full of Pryde, *from* Gude and Godlie Ballatis *(c. 1640)*

THE LAND

The tenancy is bad, but the devil is in the sub-tenancy.

Gaelic proverb

. . . land of the omnipotent No.

Alan Bold (1943–1998) A Memory of Death

Scotland the wee, crêche of the soul,
of thee I sing,
land of the millionaire draper, whisky vomit
and the Hillman Imp.

Tom Buchan (1931–1995), Scotland the Wee

The summits of the highest are mostly destitute of earth;
and the huge naked rocks, being just above the heath,
produce the disagreeable appearance of a scabbed head . . .
To cast one's eye from an eminence toward a group of
them, they appear still one above the other, fainter and
fainter, according to the aerial perspective, and the whole of
a dismal gloomy brown drawing upon a dirty purple; and
most disagreeable of all when the heath is in bloom.

Edmund Burt (c. 1695–1755), Letters from a Gentleman
in the North of Scotland *(1728–37), on the Scottish
mountains*

And well I know within that bastard land
Hath Wisdom's goddess never held command:
A barren soil where nature's germs, confin'd
To stern sterility can stint the mind,
Whose thistle well betrays the niggard earth,
Emblem of all to whom the land gives birth;
Each genial influence nurtured to resist,

A land of meanness, sophistry, and mist.

Lord Byron (1788–1824), The Curse of Minerva

Land of polluted river,
Bloodshot eyes and sodden liver,
Land of my heart forever,
Scotland the Brave.

Billy Connolly (1942–), quoted in Jonathan Margolis, The
Big Yin *(1994)*

. . . pre-commercial Scotland, a land of brigands and
bigots.

Norman Douglas (1868–1952), Siren Land

. . . the Scots countryside itself, fathered between a kailyard
and a bonny brier bush in the lee of a house with green
shutters.

Lewis Grassic Gibbon (James Leslie Mitchell, 1901–35),
Sunset Song

We are the men
Who own your glen
Though you won't see us there –
In Edinburgh clubs
And Guildford pubs
We insist how much we care.

John McGrath (1935–), The Cheviot, the Stag, and the
Black, Black Oil

All you folks are off your head
I'm getting rich from your sea bed.
I'll go home when I see fit

All I'll leave is a heap of shit.

John McGrath, The Cheviot, the Stag, and the Black, Black Oil

My blessing with the foxes dwell,
For that they hunt the sheep so well.
Ill fare the sheep, a grey-fac'd nation
That swept our hills with desolation.

Duncan Bàn MacIntyre (1724–1812), Song to the Foxes, *from Gaelic*

. . . their wizened little country

Alastair Reid, Whereabouts *(1987)*

There's nought in the Highlands but syboes and leeks,
And long-legged callants gaun wantin' the breeks.

Sir Walter Scott (1771–1832), David Gellatley's song, from Waverley

This is the land God gave to Andy Stewart.

Iain Crichton Smith (1928–1998), The White Air of March

THE LANGUAGES

That laddie has clean tint his Scotch, and found nae English.

Said by Lord Braxfield (1722–1799) of Francis Jeffrey, later to be editor of the Edinburgh Review, *when he came back from Oxford University*

Great the blindness and the sinful darkness and ignorance and evil will of those who teach, write and foster the Gaelic speech; for to win for themselves the empty rewards of the world, they both choose and use more and more to make vain and misleading tales, lying and worldly, of the Tuath de Dannan, of fighting men and champions, of Fionn MacCumhal and his heroes, and many more whom now I will not number.

John Carswell, Kirk Superintendent of Argyll (fl. mid–16th century), Introduction to a Gaelic translation of the Liturgy of the English Congregation at Geneva, *from Gaelic*

When Andrew Melville, later the leader of the Presbyterian reformers, became professor of Latin at the University of Geneva, 'his Scottish stubbornness, in defending his own pronunciation of Greek, roused the wrath of the professor of that language, who was a native of Greece. *'Vos Scotti, vos barbari!'* he indignantly exclaimed, *'docebitis nos Graecos pronunciationem linguae nostrae, scilicet?'* (You barbarian Scots, will you teach us Greeks the way to speak our own language, then?')

John Edgar, History of Early Scottish Education *(1893)*

'Learn English!' he exclaimed, 'no, never, it was my trying to learn that language that spoiled my Scots.

Dr John Leyden (1775–1811), quoted in John Reith, The Life of Dr John Leyden.
On his arrival at Bombay, Leyden had been asked to speak 'English'.

. . . none can more sincerely wish a total extinction of the Scottish *colloquial* dialect than I do, for there are few *modern* Scoticisms which are not barbarisms.

John Pinkerton (1758–1826), Preface to Ancient Scottish Poems *(1786)*

Many people think that Scots possesses a rich vocabulary, but this is a view not wholly borne out by a close examination ... It is as if the Doric had been invented by a cabal of scandal-mongering beldams, aided by a council of observant gamekeeepers.

George Malcolm Thomson, The Re-Discovery of Scotland *(1928)*

THE LAW

If the Lord Chancellor knew only a little law, he would know a little of everything.

Anonymous comment on Lord Brougham (1778–1868), in G.W.E. Russell, Collections and Recollections

A great deal rests on this gentleman's credibility. He is a Jew and may be an atheist. We are honest Scots. What faith can we put in this 'gentleman's' words?

Advocate for the defence in the trial for murder of the trades unionist Alfred French, quoted in Peter Slowe, Manny Shinwell *(1993), referring to Emmanuel Shinwell, a key witness, and later a senior Labour politician*

'Ye're a verra clever chiel', man, but ye wad be nane the waur o' a hanging.'

Alleged remark by Lord Braxfield (1722–1799), to a defendant, quoted in J.G. Lockhart, Memoirs of the Life of Sir Walter Scott *(1837–38)*

Muckle he made o' that – he was hanget.

Lord Braxfield (1722–1799), quoted by Lord Cockburn in

Memorials of His Time *(1856), a* sotto-voce *comment, during a political trial, on the remark that Jesus Christ also was a reformer*

A fig for those by law protected!
Liberty's a glorious feast!
Courts for cowards were erected,
Churches built to please the priest.

Robert Burns (1759–1796), The Jolly Beggars

When Lord Meadowbank was yet Mr Maconochie, he one day approached his facetious professional brother, John Clerk of Eldin, and after telling him he had prospects of being raised to the bench, asked him to suggest what title he should adopt.
'Lord Preserve Us,' said Clerk, and moved off.

Robert Ford, Thistledown *(1901)*

On a change of ministry, Henry Erskine was appointed to follow Henry Dundas as Lord Advocate. On the morning of his appointment, he met Dundas in the Parliament House . . . Erskine remarked that he must be off to order his silk gown.
''Tis not worth your while,' said Dundas, 'for the short time you'll want it, you had better borrow mine.'
'I have no doubt your gown,' replied Erskine, 'is made to fit *any party;* but however short may be my time in office, it shall not be said that Henry Erskine put on the *abandoned habits* of his predecessor.'

Robert Ford, Thistledown

God help the people who have such judges.

Charles James Fox (1749–1806), on the Scottish Court of Session, at the time of the political trials of the 1790s

'Fare ye a' weel, ye bitches.'

Lord Kames (1696–1782), to his fellow-judges, on leaving the Court of Session. 'Bitch' appears to have been applicable to either sex; see one of Burns's Epitaphs

A judge has sentenced himself to a suicide's grave?
– The nearest to a just sentence any judge ever gave.

Hugh MacDiarmid (C.M. Grieve, 1892–1978), A Judge Commits Suicide

An advocate complaining to his friend, an eminent legal functionary of the last century, that his claims to a judgeship had been overlooked, added acrimoniously, 'and I can tell you they might have got a *waur,*' to which the only answer was a grave *'Whaur?'*

Dean E.B. Ramsay (1793–1872), Reminiscences of Scottish Life and Character

. . . that bastard verdict, 'Not Proven'. I hate that Caledonian *medium quid.* One who is not proven guilty is innocent in the eye of the law.

Sir Walter Scott (1771–1832), Journal

Here enter not Attorneys, Barristers,
Nor bridle-champing Law-practitioners:
Clerks, Commissaries, Scribes nor Pharisees,
Wilful disturbers of the people's ease . . .
Your salary is at the gibbet-foot:

Go drink there.

Sir Thomas Urquhart (1611–1660), Translation from Rabelais, Gargantua and Pantagruel

MANNERS

. . . my fellow-passenger in the railway, took it into his head to smile very visibly when I laid off my white broadbrim, and suddenly produced out of my pocket my grey Glengarry . . . I looked straight into his smiling face and eyes, with a look which I suppose enquired of him, 'Miserable ninth part of the fraction of a tailor, art thou sure thou hast a right to smile at me?' The smile instantly died into another expression of emotion.

Thomas Carlyle (1795–1881), Letter to his wife

John Clerk was arguing a Scotch appeal case before the House of Lords. His client claimed the use of a millstream by prescriptive right. Mr Clerk spoke broad Scotch, and argued that 'the *watter* had run that way for forty years. Indeed, naebody kenned how long, and why should his client now be deprived of the *watter,*' etc. The Chancellor, much amused at the pronunciation of the Scottish advocate, asked him, in rather a bantering tone, 'Mr Clerk, do you spell water in Scotland with two t's?'
Clerk was a little nettled at this hit at his national accent, and answered, 'Na, my lord, we dinna spell water with twa t's; but we spell *mainners* wi' twa n's.'

Alexander Hislop, The Book of Scottish Anecdote *(1883), on John Clerk (1757–1832)*

The Rev. Donald Maclean, minister of Oa in Argyll in the

early 20th century, was notoriously indolent in his duties. One of his parishioners, Lachlan McNeil Weir, returned from an appendix operation in Glasgow, went to the church for the Sunday service and found it deserted. He went inside and rang the bell. Presently the minister appeared, furious and indignant. Seeing Weir, he shouted:

'They took the guts oot o' ye in Glesga, but they didna take the cheek!'

From Colin Macdonald, Highland Journey, *1943*

MEDICINE, HYGIENE AND DOCTORS

Did he dee a natural death, or was the doctor sent for?

Annandale saying, quoted in Charles Rodgers, Familiar Illustrations of Scottish Life *(1866)*

My curse upon your venom'd stang
That shoots my tortur'd gums alang,
And thro' my lug gies sic a twang
Wi' gnawing vengeance.

Robert Burns (1759–1796), Address to the Toothache

I have been far too frequently threatened by lunatics in and out of prison to worry about this lot.

Dr James Devon, force-feeder of suffragette prisoners, on his critics, from Leah Leneman, A Guid Cause: The Women's Suffrage Movement in Scotland *(1991)*

Whenever patients come to I,
I physics, bleeds and sweats 'em;
If after that they choose to die,
What's that to me? I *letts 'em.*

Thomas, Lord Erskine (1750–1823), Epigram on Dr John Lettsom

Doctors, like mini-cab drivers, are the other idiots to whom we entrust our lives.

James Kennaway (1928–68), The Kennaway Papers

Soap and water . . . have never found much favour in these parts . . . That anyone should want even one bath a week, they consider extraordinary: that anyone should desire a bath on two consecutive days, is, to them, indicative of some regrettable abnormality, if not actually a sign of daftness.

Alasdair Alpin MacGregor, The Western Isles *(1949)*

Most native-born doctors indulge in a bit of poaching, a favourite activity of peasantry. The urge to poach is in the blood.

Alasdair Alpin MacGregor, The Western Isles

MEN

Can spirit from the tomb, or fiend from Hell
More hateful, more malignant be, than Man?

Joanna Baillie (1762–1851), Orra

Every man who is high up loves to think he has done it himself: and the wife smiles, and lets it go at that.

Sir J.M. Barrie (1860–1937), What Every Woman Knows

What is man? a foolish baby;

Vainly strives, and fights, and frets;
Demanding all, deserving nothing,
One small grave is all he gets.

Thomas Carlyle (1795–1881), Cui Bono

But anyhow it wasn't a woman who betrayed Jesus with a kiss.

Catherine Carswell (1879–1946), The Savage Pilgrimage

Men, even the good ones, are kittle cattle; God didn't give them much sense, and it's the woman's job to make the best of them

O. Douglas (Anna Buchan, 1877–1948), Jane's Parlour

The curse of Scotland is these wee hard men. I used to blame the English for our mediocrity. I thought they had colonised us by sheer cunning. They aren't very cunning. They've got more confidence and money than we have, so they can afford to lean back and smile while our own wee hard men hammer Scotland down to the same dull level as themselves.

Alasdair Gray, 1982 Janine *(1984)*

Says she, 'Guid men I've kistit twa,
But a change o' deils is lichtsome, lass.'

Violet Jacob (1863–1946), A Change o' Deils

. . . men were just a perfect nuisance, wasn't that so, now?

Jessie Kesson (1915–1994), A Glitter of Mica

Two characteristics of the people, which the stranger to the Western Isles is swift to observe, certainly so far as the male population is concerned, are laziness and drunkennness.

Alasdair Alpin MacGregor, The Western Isles *(1949)*

Mr ——, in the Kyle,
Ca'd me a common —— :
But if he hadna tried himsel',
He wadna be so sure.

Isobel Pagan (1741–1821), Lines on Mr –

The Scarlet Whore, indeed, they snarl at,
But like right well a whore in scarlet

Allan Ramsay (1686–1758), Epistle to Mr H. S. at London

My mother asked a somewhat rhetorical question: how do
you keep men happy? 'You have to feed 'em at both ends,'
replied my grandmother.

Muriel Spark (1918–), Curriculum Vitae

PERSONALITIES

She kept a stir in tower and trench –
That brawling, boisterous Scottish wench;
Came I early, came I late,
I found Agnes at the gate.

*Anonymous, The Earl of Salisbury's Valediction to Black
Agnes, Countess of Dunbar, in 1338*

O Allison Gross, that lives in yon tower,
The ugliest witch in the north countrie.

Anonymous, Allison Gross *(16th century ballad)*

He is weil kend, John of the Syde,
A greater thief did never ride.

*Anonymous lines on John Armstrong of Liddesdale, quoted
in George Macdonald Fraser,* The Steel Bonnets *(1971)*

Sir James Stewart, thou'lt hing in a string;
Sir James Stewart, knave and rogue thou art,
For thou ne'er had a true heart
To God or King:
Sir James Stewart, thou'lt hing in a string.

*Anonymous Jacobite verse against Sir James Stewart (died
1713), Lord Advocate*

Here lies Durham
But Durham lies not here.

Epitaph for Mr Durham of Largo, a noted exaggerator

Bodach an t-siapuinn, The Old Fellow of the Soap.

*Gaelic nickname for Lord Leverhulme, one-time proprietor
of Lewis and Harris*

 . . . Michael Scott, who verily knew well
The lightsome play of every magic fraud.

Dante Alighieri (1265–1321), The Inferno, *on a notable
Scots 'wizard' of the Middle Ages*

If he were a horse, no-one would buy him: with that eye,
no-one could answer for his temper.

*Walter Bagehot (1826–1877), on Lord Brougham
(1778–1868), the Lord Chancellor, in* Biographical Studies

David Hume ate a swinging great dinner,
And grew every day fatter and fatter;
And yet the great bulk of a sinner
Said there was neither spirit not matter.

James Beattie (1735–1803), On the Author of the Treatise
of Human Nature

With the publication of his Private Papers in 1952, he
committed suicide twenty-five years after his death.

Lord Beaverbrook (1879–1964) on Earl Haig (1861–1928),
British Commander-in-Chief in the First World War

He wasn't a one-to-one man in the pub . . . He might let you
tug the hem of his garment once in a while, but that was all.
He was an élitist, a platform man.

John Bellany, on Hugh MacDiarmid, quoted in John
McEwen, John Bellany *(1994)*

An ugly, cross-made, splay-footed, shapeless, little
dumpling of a fellow.

Blackwood's Magazine, *anonymous description of Lord*
Macaulay (1800–1859)

The folks are green, it's oft been said,
Of that you'll find no trace:
There's seasoned wood in every head,
And brass in every face.

Look smart, and keep your eyes about,
Their tricks will make you grin;
The Barrhead coach will take you out,
The folks will take you in.

Jamie Blue (James McIndoe), Queer Folk at the Shaws *(c.*
1820)

Of lordly acquaintance you boast,
And of dukes that you dined with yestreen:
An insect's an insect at most.
Though it crawl on the curls of a queen.

Robert Burns (1759–1796), The Toadeater

That there is falsehood in his looks,
I must and will deny:
They tell their master is a knave,
And sure they do not lie.

Robert Burns, On Hearing It Asserted Falsehood is
Expressed in the Rev Dr Babington's Very Looks

She's bow-hough'd, she's hen-shinn'd,
Ae limpin' leg a hand-breed shorter;
She's twisted right, she's twisted left,
To balance fair in ilka quarter.

Robert Burns, Willie Wastle

'This gentleman is the best judge of the value of his own life.'

*Said by Robert Burns of a wealthy merchant who gave
a sailor a shilling for rescuing him from Greenock Harbour*

It was very good of God to let Carlyle and Mrs Carlyle
marry one another and so make only two people miserable
instead of four.

Samuel Butler (1835–1902)

A narrow, bitter, unreasonable being, eaten up with his own
conceit, consumed with his own petty arrogance, and
pursued from day to day, and year to year, by an unrelenting
bee in his bonnet.

Winston Churchill on D.C. Thomson, speech in Dundee, November 1922

Silly, snobbish, lecherous, tipsy . . . he needed Johnson as an ivy needs an oak.

Cyril Connolly, The Evening Colonnade, *1990, on James Boswell*

So fat and Buddhistic and nasal that that a dear friend described him as an animated adenoid.

Norman Douglas (1868–1952), quoted in R. A. Cassell, Ford Madox Ford *(1961), on the novelist Ford Madox Ford*

Madame, ye hev a dangerouss Dog.

William Dunbar (c. 1460–c. 1520), On James Dog, Kepar of the Quenis Wardrop, *a complaint to Queen Margaret about her wardrobe master.*

'There you go for a damned cowardly Italian!'

Attributed to Lord Elcho (1721–1787), as shouted to Prince Charles Edward Stuart as he withdrew from the battle at Culloden, April 16th, 1746), quoted in Sir Walter Scott (1771–1832), Journal, *February 1826*

Weill, gin they arena deid, it's time they were.

Robert Garioch (Robert Garioch Sutherland, 1919–1981), Elegy, *on Edinburgh worthies of his youth*

The 'heroic young queen' in question had the face, mind, manners and morals of a well-intentioned but hysterical poodle.

Lewis Grassic Gibbon (James Leslie Mitchell, 1901–1935),

Scottish Scene, *on Mary, Queen of Scots*

When one says of another man that he is the most arrogant man in the world, it is only to say he is very arrogant; but when one says it of Lord Kames, it is an absolute truth.

David Hume (1711–1776), quoted in James Boswell (1740–1795), Journal

Allan Ramsay, the poet, lived for a time in a remarkable house of octagonal shape on the Castle hill of Edinburgh. He was very proud of the building, and regarded it has having exceptional beauty. Showing it one day to his friend Lord Elibank, the poet said his friends had told him it resembled a goose pie. To which Lord Elibank commented: 'Indeed, Allan, now that I see you in it, I think the term is very properly applied.'

Gordon Irving, The Wit of the Scots *(1969)*

O Knox he was a bad man
he split the Scottish mind.
The one half he made cruel
and the other half unkind.

Alan Jackson (1938–), Knox

He has an attractive voice and a highly unattractive bottom. In his concert performances he now spends more time wagging the latter than exercising the former.

Clive James on Rod Stewart (1948–)

I smell you in the dark.

Samuel Johnson (1709–1784) to James Boswell

Though thou're like Judas, an apostate black,
In the resemblance thou dost one thing lack;
When he had gotten his ill-purchased pelf,
He went away and wisely hanged himself:
This thou may do at last, but yet I doubt
If thou hast any bowels to gush out.

Charles Lamb (1775–1834), Epigram on Sir James
Mackintosh *(1765–1832)*

You can't know Burns unless you hate the Lockharts and all
the estimable bourgeois and upper classes as he really did –
the narrow-gutted pigeons... Oh, why doesn't Burns
come to life again, and really salt them?

*D.H. Lawrence (1885–1930), letter to Donald Carswell,
1927, after reading Lockhart's* Life of Burns

The Judas of his country... the bane of Scotland in general.

George Lockhart of Carnwath (1673–1731), Memoirs
Concerning the Affairs of Scotland, *on the first Earl of Stair*

Ablachs, and scrats, and dorbels o' a' kinds
Aye'd drob me wi' their puir eel-dronin' minds,
Wee drochlin' craturs drutling their bit thochts
The dorty bodies! Feech! Nae Sassunach drings
'll daunton me.

Hugh McDiarmid (C. M. Grieve, 1892–1978), Gairmscoile,
on some contemporary verse-writers

... the whole gang of high mucky-mucks, famous
fatheads, old wives of both sexes, stuffed shirts, hollow
men with headpieces stuffed with straw, bird-wits, lookers-
under-beds, trained seals, creeping Jesuses, Scots Wha
Ha'evers, village idiots, policemen, leaders of white-mouse

factions and noted connoisseurs of bread and butter . . . and all the touts and toadies and lickspittles of the English Ascendancy, and their infernal womenfolk.

Hugh McDiarmid, Lucky Poet, *on his literary and political opponents*

. . . a paladin in mental fight with the presence of a Larry the Lamb.

Hugh MacDiarmid, Lucky Poet, *on Edwin Muir (1887–1959)*

Here's your likeness again:
a wisp-headed scowler,
without hat or wig,
without headpiece or crest,
you're plucked bald and bare;
with mange at your elbows
and the scratch-marks of itch at your arse.

Duncan Bàn MacIntyre (1724–1812), Song for the Tailor

The laird's nae what you could call very intelligent. There's naething in him except what he puts in with a spoon.

R.F. Mackenzie, A Search for Scotland *(1989)*

Canker'd, cursed creature, crabbed, corbit kittle,
Buntin-ars'd, beugle-back'd, bodied like a beetle;
Sarie-shitten, shell-padock, ill-shapen shoit,
Kid-bearded gennet, all alike great
Fiddle-douped, flindrikin, fart of a man,
Wa worth the, wanwordie, wanshapen wran.

Sir Thomas Maitland, Satire upon Sir Niel Laing, *c. 1556*

The fattest hog in Epicurus' sty.

William Mason, An Heroic Epistle to Sir William Chambers, *on David Hume (1711–1776)*

Lovat's head i' the pat,
Horns and a' the gither,
We'll mak brose o' that
An' gie the swine their supper.

Hugh Miller (1802–1856), Notes and Legends of the North of Scotland, *quoting a local rhyme on Lord Lovat who was executed in 1746*

In the furor which followed Boswell's *Life of Johnson,* he was asked what he thought of Boswell. He replied, 'Before I read his book I thought he was a Gentleman who had the misfortune to be mad: I now think he is a madman who has the misfortune not to be a Gentleman.'

Quoted of Lord Monboddo (1714–1799), in E.L. Cloyd, James Burnett, Lord Monboddo *(1972)*

He comes out of the shop
with the latest fashion from France
and the fine clothes worn on his person
yesterday with no little satisfaction
are tossed into a corner

Roderick Morison (c. 1656–c. 1714), Oran dho MhacLeòid Dhùn Bheagan (Song on MacLeod of Dunvegan), *the young wastrel chief*

the archetypal Scotch crawler.

Tom Nairn (1932–), The Timeless Girn, *in O.D. Edwards,* A Claim of Right for Scotland *(1989), on Andrew Neil*

Jemmy . . . in recording the noble growlings of the Great Bear, thought not of his own Scotch snivel.

Christopher North (John Wilson, 1785–1854), Noctes Ambrosianae, *on James Boswell (1740–1795)*

I was present in a large company at dinner, when Bruce was talking away. Someone asked him what musical instruments were used in Abyssinia. Bruce hesitated, not being prepared for the question, and at last said, 'I think I saw one *lyre* there.' George Selwyn whispered his next man, 'Yes, and there is one less since he left the country.'

Recorded of James Bruce of Kinnaird (1730–1794), author of A Journey to the Source of the Nile, *in John Pinkerton,* Walpoliana

When Carlyle's thunder had been followed by his wife's sparkle, their sardonic host said in a half-soliloquy which was intended to be audible: 'As soon as that man's tongue stops, that woman's begins.'

Quoted of Samuel Rogers in Francis Espinasse, Literary Recollections and Sketches *(1893)*

Sellar, daith has ye in his grip;
Ye needna think he'll let ye slip.
Justice ye've earned, and, by the Book,
A warm assize ye winna jouk.
The fires ye lit to gut Strathnaver,
Ye'll feel them noo – and roast forever.

Lines on Patrick Sellar, the Duke of Sutherland's factor, acquitted in court for his actions in the Sutherland Clearances. Recorded in 1958 from Andrew Stewart, Melness, Sutherland, and noted in Hamish Henderson, The Armstrong Nose: Selected Letters of Hamish Henderson, *edited by Alec Findlay (1996).*

Lord Charlemont described the expression of his mouth as imbecilic, that of his eyes as vacant, and the corpulence of his frame as befitting rather a 'turtle-eating alderman' than a philosopher.

Alastair Smart, The Life and Art of Allan Ramsay *(1952), on David Hume (1711–1776)*

John Paul Jones demonstrates, better than anybody, that endearing protean quality of the Scot, to be all things to all men, providing the price is right.

W. Gordon Smith, Mr Jock *(1978), on John Paul Jones, Scottish-born 'father' of the U.S. Navy*

The grating scribbler! whose untuned Essays
Mix the Scotch Thistle with the English Bays;
By either Phoebus preordained to ill,
The hand prescribing, or the flattering quill,
Who doubly plagues, and boasts two Arts to kill.

J.M. Smythe, One Epistle to Mr Alexander Pope, *on the doctor-poet John Arbuthnot (1667–1735). Arbuthnot could produce a fine insult himself: see* Epitaphs.

. . . up to his death three years before, she had been living with Lord Alfred Douglas, the fatal lover of Oscar Wilde, an arrangement which I imagine would satisfy any woman's craving for birth control . . . I used to think it a pity that her mother rather than she had not thought of birth control . . . I was young and pretty; she had totally succumbed to the law of gravity.

Muriel Spark (1918–), Curriculum Vitae, *on Marie Stopes, the Edinburgh-born pioneer of birth control*

He's gone to Heaven, no doubt, but he won't like God.

Robert Louis Stevenson (1850–1894) on Matthew Arnold (1822–1888)

There is a certain class of clever Scotsmen, who complete their education at the University of Oxford, with results not very creditable to themselves, or to the country of their origin . . . possessed with an innate flunkeyism which leads them, not merely to bow down to and humbly accept Anglian ideas and Anglicising influences; but also with these, a desire to belittle the country which gave them birth, and to sneer at Scottish ways.

T.D. Wanliss in The Thistle *(December 1912), on Professor J.H. Millar of Edinburgh University, quoted in H.J. Hanham*, Scottish Nationalism *(1969)*

One day I met Gilbert Noble, who is married to Dunkie's Jock's adopted daughter. With him was Joe Maclean, who said to me, 'Do you mind when you put the paraffin on the hen-house?' Gilbert Noble was furious at him and said, 'Joe, you should have left that alane.'
He did not worry me, but I replied, 'Yes, and do you mind when you used to piss your breeks when you were a great big loon who should have known better, and the lave of the bairns in the school were scumfished with stink?'

Christian Watt (1833–1923), The Christian Watt Papers

He was so monstrously ill-favoured as to possess some of the attractiveness of a gargoyle. He had neither dignity, nor what a Roman would have called gravity. As Lord Chancellor he distinguished himself by belching from the Woolsack.

Esmé Wingfield Stratford, on Lord Brougham (1778–1868), Lord Chancellor of Great Britain

As a poet Scott *cannot* live ... What he writes in the way
of natural description is merely rhyming nonsense.

*William Wordsworth (1770–1850), conversation reported
by Mrs Davy, 1844, on Sir Walter Scott*

With an expression half-bovine and half-sheeplike he stares
out of the screen in such a way as to leave us all uncertain
whether he wants to cut our throats or lick our boots.

Peregrine Worsthorne, quoted in Jonathon Green,
Dictionary of Insults *(1995) on Andrew Neil (1949–)*

PLACES

Oh, —— is a dirty hole,
A kirk without a steeple,
A midden heap at every door,
And damned uncivil people.

*Traditional rhyme of abuse to the next town; supply the
place of your choice*

Polomint City

East Kilbride, famous for its many roundabouts

Fish guts and stinkin' herrin
Are bread and milk for an Eyemouth bairn

Old rhyme

Glasgow is not for me.
I do not see the need for such a crowd.

Anonymous Gaelic poet, quoted in Alasdair Maclean, Night
Falls on Ardnamurchan *(1989)*

'Heaven seems vera little improvement on Glesga,' a Glasgow man is said to have murmured, after death, to a friend who had predeceased him. 'Man, this is no heaven,' the other replied.

Traditional

It's a shame over there –
So many Lowlanders in Inverness;
Even if there weren't so many,
I wouldn't have missed a few.

Comment on the capital of the Highlands, from Gaelic

What's Motherwell famous for?
Coal and steel.
And what's Hamilton famous for?
Stealin' coal.

One-time Motherwell saying

Musselburgh was a burgh
When Edinburgh was nane;
And Musselburgh will be a burgh
When Edinburgh is gane.

Traditional Musselburgh rhyme

A Paisley screwdriver.

Traditional Glaswegian definition of a hammer

Oh Rhynie is a cauld place,
It doesna suit a Lowland loon!
And Rhynie is a cauld clay hole,
It is na like my father's toun.

Anonymous, Linten Lowren

This bloody town's a bloody cuss,
No bloody train, no bloody bus,
And no-one cares for bloody us,
In bloody Orkney . . .
No bloody sports, no bloody games,
No bloody fun; the bloody dames
Won't even give their bloody names,
In bloody Orkney.

Hamish Blair, Bloody Orkney *(composed by a serviceman during World War II), from Arnold Silcock,* Verse and Worse *(1952)*

There's nothing here but Hielan' pride
And Hielan' scab and hunger;
If Providence has sent me here,
'Twas surely in an anger.

Robert Burns (1759–1796), Epigram on the Inn at Inveraray

. . . this accursed, stinking, reeky mass of stones and lime and dung.

Thomas Carlyle (1795–1881), Letter to his brother John, February 1821, on Edinburgh

At Oban of discomfort one is sure;
Little the difference whether rich or poor,

Arthur Hugh Clough (1819–1861), Mari Magno, The Lawyer's Second Tale

If Dingwall was in its ordinary state, it must be an excellent place for sleeping away a life in.

Lord Cockburn (1779–1854), Circuit Journeys *(1852)*

Dundee, the palace of Scottish blackguardism, unless perhaps Paisley be entitled to contest this honour with it.

Lord Cockburn, Circuit Journeys

Dundee, certainly now, and for many years past, the most blackguard place in Scotland . . . a sink of atrocity . . . A Dundee criminal, especially if a lady, may be known, without any evidence about character, by the intensity of the crime, the audacious bar air, and the parting curses.

Lord Cockburn, Circuit Journeys

Crianlarich is the most signposted nowhere on the planet.
Jim Crumley (1947–), Gulfs of Blue Air

Your burgh of beggaris is ane nest,
To shout the swengouris will nocht rest,
All honest folk they do molest
So piteously they cry and rame.

William Dunbar (c. 1460– c. 1520), Satire on Edinburgh
(Over five hundred years later, in 1998, the Edinburgh City Council was still trying to expel beggars from the city centre)

Glasgow, that damned sprawling evil town

G.S. Fraser (1915–1980), Meditation of a Patriot

. . . this sad old city – you see her pinioned by her judges and preyed on by their wig-lice, that countless vermin of lawyerlings, swollen and small. You see her left in squalor by her shopkeepers, the bawbee-worshipping bailie-bodies, and pushioned by her doctors; you hear her dulled by the blithers of her politicians and deived by the skreigh of the newsboy-caddies who squabble at their heels, and you know how she has been paralysed by the piffle of her professors, more than half-doited or driven into alternate hidebound or hysteric nightmares by every chilly dogmatism, every flaring hell-blast imagined by three centuries and more of diabologic Divines.

Sir Patrick Geddes (1854–1932), Letter to R.B. Cunninghame Graham (August 1909), from P. Boardman, The Worlds of Patrick Geddes *(1978), on Edinburgh*

Aberdeen . . . a thin-lipped peasant woman who has borne eleven and buried nine . . . Union Street has as much warmth in its face as a dowager duchess asked to contribute to the Red International Relief.

Lewis Grassic Gibbon (James Leslie Mitchell, 1901–1935), on Aberdeen, in Scottish Scene *(1934)*
Dundee, a frowsy fisherwife given to gin and infanticide.

Lewis Grassic Gibbon, Scottish Scene

Edinburgh . . . a disappointed spinster with a hare-lip and inhibitions.

Lewis Grassic Gibbon, Scottish Scene

Glasgow . . . the vomit of a cataleptic commercialism.

Lewis Grassic Gibbon (James Leslie Mitchell, 1901–1935), The Thirteenth Disciple

Stonehaven . . . home of the poverty toffs, folks said, where you might live in sin as much as you pleased but were damned to hell if you hadn't a white sark.

Lewis Grassic Gibbon, Cloud Howe

If the world comes to an end, Edinburgh will never notice.

Jo Grimond (1913–1996), interview in The Scotsman, *27 October 1979*

Hamilton is notoriously a dull place; if a joke finds its way into our neighbourhood, it is looked upon with as much surprise as a comet would be.

The Hamilton Hedgehog, October 1856

Then suddenly the sun was snuffed
Behind a sooty cloud,
And night let fall on Glasgow Green
Its sulphur-stinking shroud.

Iain Hamilton (1920–1986), News of the World

As every schoolboy knows, Edinburgh is redolent with history, which in the case of Scotland consists mainly of people knifing one another or blowing up one another's bedrooms.

Cliff Hanley (1922–1999)

What bloody shits the Dundeans must be.

T.E. Lawrence, letter to Sir Edward Marsh, November 1922. They had failed to re-elect Winston Churchill as their MP.

Dundee . . . As men have made it, ist stands today perhaps the completest monument in the country of human folly, avarice and selfishness.

Fionn MacColla (T.D. Macdonald, 1906–1975), in George Scott-Moncrieff, Scottish Country *(1936)*

Stornoway is a town distinguished by what Shakespeare described as 'a very ancient and fish-like smell'.

Alasdair Alpin MacGregor, The Western Isles *(1949)*

A town with guts – you see some on the pavement.

Forbes Masson (1964–) and Alan Cumming (1965–), Glasgow Song

Glasgow has been a great home for the people of Inverness, who used to come down with the hayseed in their boots and the heather sticking out of their ears.

James Maxton (1885–1946), to the MP for Inverness, in the House of Commons, 1934, quoted in G. McAllister, James Maxton: Portrait of a Rebel *(1935)*

No jokes of any kind are understood here, I have not made one for two months, and if I feel one coming I shall bite my tongue.

James Clerk Maxwell (1831–1879), on being elected to the Chair of Mathematics at Marischal College, Aberdeen

Cumbernauld in a kilt.

Tom Morton, on Inverness

Dolphinsludge.

Tom Morton's name for Inverness

Words cannot express how horrible Oban is . . . tacky beyond belief, full of disgusting shops selling Highland dancer dolls.

Tom Morton, Spirit of Adventure *(1985)*

Dumfries. . . a blowsy, overgrown country town.

Edwin Muir (1887–1959), Scottish Journey

The gap on the map.

David Mundell MSP, 21 March 2000, referring to how Dumfries and Galloway is seen from outside

Inverkip is so rough they put a date-stamp on your head when they mug you so they don't do you twice in the one day.

Chic Murray (1919–1985), quoted in A. Yule, The Chic Murray Bumper Fun Book *(1991)*

Most of the denizens wheeze, snuffle and exhale a sort of snozzling whnoff, whnoff, apparently through a hydrophile sponge.

Ezra Pound (1885–1972), on Edinburgh, quoted in Hugh MacDiarmid, Lucky Poet *(1943)*

Girvan – a cauld, cauld place. Naebuddy o' ony conse-quence was ever born here.

'Robin Ross', in The Chiel, *January 1885, quoted in William Donaldson,* The Language of the People *(1989)*

St Monans. . . has been quaintly taken over, like many such, by functionless foreigners . . . their seaside homes have been prettified by the National Trust, shot right up out of the price range of local buyers, inhabited briefly by effete antique dealers and fifth-rate television personalities. . .

Christopher Rush, A Twelvemonth and a Day *(1985)*

You cut your finger and by the time news gets to the end of the road it's become an amputation.

Local resident, on Kirkcudbright, quoted in The Scotsman, *September 1999*

. . . I could see the lights of Kirkwall twinkling across the water, miles to the south-east. 'Ah,' I would think to myself, 'there's that Babylon of a place, full of distraction and debauchery.'

Will Self, The Rousay Effect

The saturnine Heart of Midlothian, never mine.

Muriel Spark (1918–), on Edinburgh

This grim, grey, sea-beaten hole.

Robert Louis Stevenson (1850–1894), letter to his mother, 1868, on Anstruther

Wick is . . . the meanest of men's towns, set on what is surely the baldest of God's bays.

Robert Louis Stevenson, letter to his mother, 1868

The town is ill-built and is dirty beside,
For with water it's scantily, badly supplied . . .
And abounds so in smells that a stranger supposes
The people are very different in noses.

Thomas Stuart, Dundee *(1815)*

It was only in Aberdeen that I saw . . . the kind of tartan tight-fistedness that made me think of the average Aberdonian as a person who would gladly pick a penny out of a dunghill with his teeth.

Paul Theroux, A Kingdom by the Sea *(1983)*

I do wonder that so brave a prince as King James should be born in so stinking a town as Edinburgh in lousy Scotland.

Sir Anthony Weldon, A Perfect Guide to the People and Country of Scotland *(1617)*

Fort Augustus
Did disgust us,
And Fort William did the same.
At Letterfinlay
We fared thinly;
At Ballachulish
We looked foolish,
Wondering why we thither came

William Wordsworth (1770–1850), quoted in Robert Southey, Journal of a Tour in Scotland

POLITICS AND POLITICIANS

Brodie: No innocent blood in all his reign was shed.
Lillias: Save all Glencoe in one night murdered.
Brodie: He saved our country, and advanced our trade.
Lillias: Witness such product we from Darien had.

Anonymous, imaginary dialogue between the Laird of Brodie and Lillias Brodie, on the death of King William II (1702) from Maidment's Scottish Pasquils

Four and twenty blacklegs, working night and day,
Fed on eggs and bacon, getting double pay;
Helmets on their thick heads, bayonets gleaming bright,
If someone burst a sugar bag, the lot would die of fright.

Anonymous, student magazine of 1928, quoted in Roy M. Pinkerton, Of Chambers and Communities, in G. Donaldson, Four Centuries: Edinburgh University Life *(1983)*

This is the savage pimp without dispute
First bought his mother for a prostitute;

Of all the miscreants ever went to hell,
This villain rampant bears away the bell.

*Anonymous, 17th century, on the Duke of Lauderdale
(1616–1682), Secretary for Scotland*

The Stuarts, antient true-born race,
We must all now give over;
We must receive into their place
The mungrells of Hanover

*A Curse on The Unionists and Revolutionaries, from J.
Maidment,* Book of Scottish Pasquils *(1866)*

Our Duiks were deills, our marquesses were mad,
Our Earls were evills, our Viscounts yet more bade,
Our Lords were villains, and our Barons knaves,
Quho with our burrows did sell us for slaves

Verses on the Scottish Peers, *1706, from J. Maidment,* Book
of Scottish Pasquils *(1866)*

Auld Satan cleekit him by the spaul
And stappit him in the dub o' Hell.
The foulest fiend there daurna bide him,
The damned they wadna fry beside him.
Till the bluidy Duke cam trysting thither,
And the ae fat butcher fried the ither.

Anonymous, Jacobite verse from Cromek's Select Scottish
Songs, *on Sir John Murray of Broughton, the turncoat
Jacobite, and the Duke of Cumberland*

O Bute, if instead of contempt and odium,
You wish to obtain universal eulogium,
From your breast to your gullet transfer the blue string:

Our hearts are all yours from the very first swing.

Anonymous, 18th century, on the Earl of Bute (1713–1792),
Prime Minister

Stick to Marx, my hearty,
Damn the Labour Party

Anonymous street song, early 20th century

George Galloway, MP: 'Why do people take such an instant
dislike to me?'
Anonymous colleague: 'It saves time.'

Matthew Parris and Phil Mason, Read My Lips, *1996*

All political parties die at length of swallowing their own
lies.

John Arbuthnot (1666–1735)

. . . has not the brains of a Glasgow bailie.

H.H. Asquith (1852–1928), to David Lloyd George, quoted
in Frances Stevenson, Diary, *November 1916, on Andrew*
Bonar Law (1858–1923), former Prime Minister

He pursues us with a malignant fidelity.

Arthur James Balfour (1848–1930), on an unwanted supporter,
quoted in Winston Churchill, Great Contemporaries *(1937)*

'It's like any Parish Council . . . '

Tony Blair, on the proposed Scottish parliament,
newspaper report

I thought he was a young man of promise; but it appears he was a young man of promises.

Arthur James Balfour on Winston Churchill, quoted in Randolph Churchill, Winston Churchill, *Vol. 1*

His long lank and greasy hair made him look like an Indian squaw who had lost interest in life and had decided to let everything go . . . ended as the most popular member of the Commons . . . rather a queer ending for the apostle of 'socialism in our time'.

Colm Brogan, The Glasgow Story *(1952) on James Maxton*

No Chancellor until this has come to the House and said that because he had money available to him the rich will get the benefits and the poor will make the sacrifices.

Gordon Brown (1951–), quoted in The Observer, *May 1988, on Norman Lamont's Budget*

He was the coldest friend and the violentest enemy I ever had.

Gilbert Burnet (1643–1715), History of His Own Time, *on the first Duke of Lauderdale, Secretary for Scotland*

What force or guile could not subdue
Thro' many warlike ages,
Is wrought now by a coward few,
For hireling traitor's wages.
The English steel we could disdain,
Secure in valour's station;
But English gold has been our bane –
Such a parcel of rogues in a nation!

Robert Burns (1759–196), Such a Parcel of Rogues in a

Nation, *on those Scots bribed to support the Treaty of Union, 1707*

. . . a cursed old Jew, not worth his weight in cold bacon

Thomas Carlyle (1795–1881), on Benjamin Disraeli (1804–1881), Tory Prime Minister; recorded in Monypenny and Buckle, The Life of Benjamin D'Israeli, Lord Beaconsfield

Gladstone appears to me one of the contemptiblest men I ever looked on.

Thomas Carlyle, on William Ewart Gladstone (1809–1898), Liberal Prime Minister

I remember, when I was a child, being taken to the celebrated Barnum's Circus, which contained an exhibition of freaks and monstrosities; but the exhibit on the programme which I most desired to see was the one described as 'The Boneless Wonder'. My parents judged that the spectacle would be too revolting and demoralising for my youthful eyes, and I have waited fifty years to see The Boneless Wonder sitting on the Treasury Bench.

Winston Churchill (1874–1965), on Ramsay Macdonald (1866–1937), Labour and then National Government Prime Minister, in the House of Commons

We know that he has, more than any other man, the gift of compressing the largest number of words into the smallest amount of thought.

Winston Churchill on Ramsay Macdonald, in the House of Commons

On the day that he took the (Liberal) party by the tail, the tail dropped off, and all that remains to C.B. is the tail . . .

He is too Scotch to perceive that nobody wants him, and if he saw it he is too Scotch to go.

T.W. Crosland, The Unspeakable Scot *(1902), on Sir Henry Campbell-Bannerman (1836–1908), leader of the Liberal Party, later Prime Minister*

Wha the de'il hae we gotten for a king,
But a wee, wee German lairdie!
Allan Cunningham (1784–1842), Wha The De'il Hae We Gotten for a King

This is included on sufferance for its fame; its author was born seventy years after George I came to the throne. Like most well-known Jacobite songs, it is post-Jacobite in origin

He has all the qualifications for a great Liberal Prime Minister. He wears spats and he has a beautiful set of false teeth.

R.B. Cunninghame Graham (1852–1936), on Sir Henry Campbell-Bannerman, Prime Minister

The Prime Minister is a sustained, brazen deceiver . . . I say she is a bounder, a liar, a deceiver, a cheat and a crook.

Tam Dalyell, MP, on Mrs Margaret Thatcher, 29 October 1988

Socialism? These days? There's the tree that never grew. *Och, a shower of shites.* There's the bird that never flew.

Carol Ann Duffy (1955–), Politico

The late Oliver Brown . . . put it well. He said that when I won Hamilton you could feel a chill run along the Labour back benches looking for a spine to run up.

Winnie Ewing (1929–), Nationalist politician, quoted in Kenneth Roy, Conversations in a Small Country *(1989)*

The Honourable Lady was once an egg, and people on both sides of this House greatly regret its fertilisation.

Sir Nicholas Fairbairn (1933–1995), on Mrs Edwina Currie, during the salmonella scare

It is fit only for the slaves who sold it.

Andrew Fletcher of Saltoun (1655–1716), comment on Scotland after the Union with England in 1707, quoted in G.W.T. Ormond, Fletcher of Saltoun *(1897)*

He had sufficient conscience to bother him, but not enough to keep him straight.

David Lloyd George (1863–1945), on Ramsay Macdonald, Labour and National Government Prime Minister (1866–1937)

A one-eyed fellow in blinkers.

David Lloyd George on Lord Rosebery (1847–1929), Liberal Prime Minister

Mr Kirkwood: What about Calton Jail, that is empty?
Duchess of Atholl: If the honourable member would like to be returned as a representative of his constituency to the Calton Jail, he is quite welcome to do so.
Mr Kirkwood: I have been there before.

Hansard, *1924, quoted in Andrew Marr,* The Battle for Scotland *(1992)*

On Hardie's first day at the House of Commons, the policeman at the gate took one look at the former miner, dressed in his ordinary working clothes and cloth cap, and asked suspiciously, 'Are you working here?'
'Yes,' replied Hardie.

'On the roof?'

'No,' said the new MP. 'On the floor.'

Quoted in C. Fadiman, The Little, Brown Book of Anecdotes, *(1985), on James Keir Hardie (1856–1915), the first Labour MP*

The Scottish Tories are an extreme case of necrophilia.

Christopher Harvie (1944–), Cultural Weapons

Jean Hamilton . . . fell out on me publiklye that I could not spell nor pronounce and then told that I was Kings Advocat and had sold the King as Judas had sold his Master, that their was a Judas heir, that I had killed Earle of Montrose . . . that tho I pretended to denye the world I had it fast in my airmes.

Archibald Johnston of Wariston (1611–1663), Diary, *June 1656*

The vast majority of Scotland's elected representatives are moral and political cowards.

James Kelman (1946–), Some Recent Attacks *(1992)*

May his guts fall out.

Norman MacCaig (1910–1996), on a Lord Provost of Edinburgh, quoted in Karl Miller, Rebecca's Vest *(1993)*

He is in fact a zombie. . . not really a Scotsman of course, but only a sixteenth part of one, and all his education and social affiliations are anti-Scottish. Sir Walter warned long ago that a Scotchman unscotched would become only a damned mischievous Englishman, and that is precisely what has happened in this case.

Hugh MacDiarmid (C.M. Grieve, 1892–1978), when

*standing as a Communist candidate against Sir Alec
Douglas-Home, in September 1964*

If I had my way
I would melt your gold payment,
Pour it into your skulls
Until it reached your boots.

Iain Lom Macdonald (c. 1620–c. 1707), Oran na Agaidh na
Aonaidh *(Song Against the Union), attacking those who
were bribed to support the Union with England*

Margaret Thatcher is not just a perpetrator of bad policies.
She is a cultural vandal. She takes the axe of her own
simplicity to the complexities of Scottish life.

*William McIlvanney (1930–), Speech to the Scottish
National Party Conference, September 1987, published in*
Surviving the Shipwreck *(1991)*

. . . you have adopted the rule and course
That Judas, your own brother, followed;
great is the scandal in your country
that such a brute did grow in it . . .
You have talked unsparingly of Scotland,
and had better have kept silent;
Were you to come to the Rough Bounds
Woe to one in your case.

Duncan Bàn MacIntyre (1724–1812), Song to John Wilkes,
*from Gaelic (Wilkes was an English politician notable for
anti-Scottish, or anti-Jacobite, sentiments)*

When Harold Macmillan, as Prime Minister, suddenly
sacked many of his Cabinet colleagues, the Lord Chancellor,
Lord Kilmuir, complained: 'A cook would have been given

more notice of his dismissal.'

'Ah,' said Macmillan, 'but good cooks are hard to find.'

Sam Galbraith, the Glaswegian minister of education and alumnus of Heidbutter High.

Robert MacNeil, The Scotsman, *23 March 2000*

I have never concealed that in my youth I was a Conservative; but never, in the depths of my igorance and degradation, was I a Liberal.

James Maxton (1885–1946), replying in the House of Commons to a member who accused him of having once been a Liberal

British 'Parliamentary cretinism' (to use Lenin's old phrase) had found its last abiding refuge within the Scottish National Party, where sectarian infantilism seems likely to keep the old thing warm until a true Dooomsday comes.

Tom Nairn (1932–), The Timeless Girn, *in O.D. Edwards,* A Claim of Right for Scotland *(1989)*

This evil mélange of decrepit Presbyterianism and imperialist thuggery, whose spirit may be savoured by a few mornings with the Edinburgh *Scotsman* and a few evenings watching Scottish television, appears to be solidly represented in the SNP.

Tom Nairn, The Three Dreams of Scottish Nationalism

I remember the time when his life would not have been worth twopence, but I urge you to do him no physical injury. It is hard, I know, for you to tolerate him in your midst, but I pray to God that you may restrain yourselves.

Father A. O'Brien, parish priest of Shettleston, on a Socialist parishioner, 1911; quoted in Ian Wood, John Wheatley

Long and lean, with the features of a kindly giraffe.

Edward Pearce on Donald Dewar, first First Minister, in Humming Birds and Hyenas

They have been on a banana-shaped learning curve and more often than not have slid down it.

The Scotsman, *editorial on members of the Scottish Parliament, September 1999*

The Right Honourable Gentleman is indebted to his memory for his jests and to his imagination for his facts.

Richard Brinsley Sheridan (1751–1816), on Henry Dundas, the Tory government's manager of Scottish affairs, in the House of Commons

(Palmerston's) manner when speaking is like a man washing his hands; the Scotch members don't know what he is doing.

Sydney Smith (1771–1845)

The Scotch Electorate is rather an incomprehensible body.

Lord Stamfordham, private secretary to King George V, letter to Winston Churchill, November 1922. Churchill had just been dumped by the electors of Dundee, having referred to his seat in 1908 as 'a life seat and cheap and easy beyond all experience'.

Labour in Scotland have been launched more often than a lifeboat.

Nicola Sturgeon MSP, August 1999

Rearrange the following into a well-known phrase or saying – prat, little, pompous – and it will immediately be evident that it is of President Lord Sir David Steel that we treat.

Gerald Warner, Scotland on Sunday, *September 1999*

REPARTEE

Reporter at door: 'Sir James Barrie, I presume?'
Sir James Barrie: 'You do.' (closes door)

A Glasgow carter, needing someone to hold his horse for a moment, asked a pompous-looking gent who happened to be passing.
'My man,' said the pompous gent, 'do you realise that I am a Bailie of this city?'
'Even if you are,' said the carter, 'surely ye widnae steal my horse.'

A prematurely white-haired man was walking down a path in a Highland glen, when he saw two girls coming towards him. As they passed, one murmured to the other:
'Snow has come early to the hills this year.'
Quick as a flash, the man replied:
'And the young cows are down in the glen already.'

From Gaelic

James Gillespie, founder of the school that bears his name, made his money out of snuff-dealing. When first he became

rich enough to buy a carriage, he asked Thomas Erskine to
suggest a motto to go with his initials on the door.
After an instant's thought, Erskine came up with this:
'Wha wad hae thocht it,
That noses had bocht it?'

. . . the Empress found some intellectual diversion in the
island. In conversation with the wife of a Caledonian named
Argentocoxus, after the treaty had been concluded, Julia
had joked with her about the sexual customs of her people,
referring to their women's freedom in having sexual
intercourse with men. The Caledonian woman showed a
biting humour in her reply: 'We fulfil the demands of nature
in a much better way than you Roman women. We have
intercourse openly with the best men – you allow
yourselves to be seduced in secret by the worst of men.'

Anthony Birley, Septimius Severus: The African Emperor
*(1971), quoting the Roman historian Dio Cassius (c. 150–c.
235), on Severus's invasion of Caledonia,* AD *208–9*

On his return from the House of Lords to the Tower, an old
woman, not very well favoured, had pressed through the
crowd and screamed in at the window of the coach, 'You'll
get that nasty head of yours chopped off, you ugly old
Scotch dog,' to which he answered, 'I believe I shall, you
ugly old English bitch.'

John Hill Burton, Life of Simon Lord Lovat *(1847), on the
trial and execution of Lord Lovat in 1747*

The medieval scholar John Scotus (c. 810–c. 877) was a
member of Charlemagne's court at Aix-la-Chapelle. On day,
as he was sitting opposite the king at meal-time, Charlemagne
inquired of him, 'What is there between *Sottum* and *Scottum*
(that is, what difference between a fool and a Scot). The

Scot's legendary reply was, 'The width of this table, Sire.'

Adapted from Arnold Fleming, The Medieval Scots Scholar in France

At a country house party, the guests were having breakfast. On the sideboard was a new patent apparatus for boiling eggs. One lady, whose garrulous conversation had already irritated another guest, was standing by him as she tried to make sense of the egg boiler. In her agitation she dropped the egg.

'Oh, I've dropped it,' she cried. 'What shall I do?'

'The usual thing,' observed the other guest, 'is to cackle.'

From John Gillespie, Humours of Scottish Life, *1904*

Jeffrey, when addressing a jury in a certain trial, had occasion to speak freely of a military officer who was a witness in the case. Having frequently described him as 'this soldier', the witness, who was present, could not restrain himself, but started up, calling out –

'Don't call me a soldier, sir; I am an officer.'

'Well, gentlemen of the jury,' proceeded Mr Jeffrey, 'this officer, who, according to his own statement, is no soldier, was the whole cause of the whole disturbance.'

Alexander Hislop, The Book of Scottish Anecdote *(1883), of Francis Jeffrey (1773–1850)*

'How had you the audacity, John,' said a Scottish laird to his servant, ' to go and tell some people that I was a mean fellow, and no gentleman?'

'Na, na, sir,' was the candid answer, 'you'll no catch me at the likes o' that. I aye *keep my thoughts to mysel'*.'

Alexander Hislop, The Book of Scottish Anecdote *(1883)*

'Is't a laddie or a lassie?' said the gardener. 'A laddie,' said the maid. 'Weel,' says he, 'I'm glad o' that, for there's ower many women in the world.' 'Hech, man,' said Jess, 'div ye no ken there's aye maist sawn o' the best crap?'

Dean E.B. Ramsay (1793–1872), Reminiscences of Scottish Life and Character

. . . it appeared that Johnson no sooner saw Smith than he attacked him for some point of his famous letter on the death of Hume. 'What did Johnson say?' was the universal enquiry. 'Why, he said,' replied Smith, with the deepest expression of resentment, 'he said, *you lie!* ''And what did you reply?' 'I said, *you* are the son of a –.' On such terms did these two great moralists meet and part

Sir Walter Scott (1771–1832), in The Life of Samuel Johnson LLD, *edited by J. W. Croker, on the meeting in Glasgow between Adam Smith and Samuel Johnson (the truth of the account has been doubted)*

She was beautifully attired in cream silk; the heavy piping and large buttons of her dress were covered in a fine check Fraser tartan. I decided 'Now I shall let you have it, I will take the wind out of your sails.' I asked what she thought she was. He replied that one must maintain standards; I told them they would be in a bonny mess if the poor disappeared overnight, and 'it will be a bad day for you when they decide to maintain standards.' He said, 'This is a democracy, with reasonable opportunity for all;' I said, 'That is the biggest load of dirt since the dung cart went round the Broch gathering the dry closets yesterday.' He was excited and started to habber.

'Please do not talk such vulgarity in the presence of my wife.'

I said to the wifie, 'As for you, madam, your heart is as cold as your backside is reputed to be.'

Christian Watt (1833–1923) The Christian Watt Papers, *edited by David Fraser. She was talking to Lord and Lady Lovat, around 1850. The local nickname for Lady Lovat was Lady Cauldock; she found the Buchan climate chilly and even in summer was reputed to wear two pairs of flannel drawers.*

Dr Taylor, the oculist, was one evening supping at William, Earl of Dumfries's, at Edinburgh. He harangued with his usual fluency and impudence, and boasted that he knew the thoughts of everybody by looking at their eyes. The first Lady Dumfries, who was hurt with his behaviour, asked him with a smile of contempt, 'Pray, sir, do you know what I am thinking?'
'Yes, madam,' said he.
'Then,' replied the countess, 'It's very safe, for I am sure you will not repeat it.'

Alexander Webster (1707–1784), quoted in Charles Rogers, Boswelliana *(1874)*

At a ceilidh in the north, the *Fear an Tighe* rose to introduce the next performer.
'Now Miss Jeannie MacLeod will give us a song,' he said.
'She's a wee whore,' came a voice from the back of the hall.
'Nevertheless,' said the *Fear an Tighe,* 'she will now give us a song.'

From Nigel Rees, The Guinness Dictionary of Jokes *(1995)*

ROYALTY, LORDS, LAIRDS AND LADIES

Do ye not know who lyes in this corner?
It's a Scots Ambassador extraordinar . . .

Ladies, I request you, keep from the Wall,
Or the Scots Ambassador will occupy you all.

Anonymous lines on the Earl of Rothes (1600–c. 1641)
John Steuart: Say no treuth
John, Lord Traquaire: A lyer honor acquyred

Anagrams made on the Earl of Traquair, 1640

Stair's neck, mynd, wife, sons, grandson and the rest,
Are wry, false, witch, pests, parricid, possest

Satyre on the Familie of Stairs, *on Sir James Dalrymple,
Viscount Stair (1619–1695), and his family, early 18th
century*

Curs'd be the Stars which did ordain
Queen Bess a maiden-life should reign;
Married, she might have brought an heir
Nor had we known a Stuart here.
Curs'd be the tribe who at Whitehall
Slew one o' th' name, and slew not all.

*Anonymous, English pasquinade against the Stewarts,
c. 1680*

A brat of an unburried Bitch,
Gott by Belzebub on a witch.

*Anonymous Epitaph on the First Earl of Stair, from
J. Maidment, Book of Scottish Pasquils (1866)*

Open your doors, you devils, and prepare
A room that's warm for honest Lady Stair.

Anonymous, Upon the Long Wished-for and Tymely Death
of the Right Honourable the Lady Stair

Thou soncie auld carle, the world hes not thy lyke,
For ladies fa' in love with thee, tho' thou be ane auld tyke.

Anonymous comment on the elderly Viscount Tarbat's marriage to the younger Countess of Wemyss (1700)

Pluto did frown, but Proserpine did smile,
Att Hell, to hear the knocks of Old Argyle.
Pluto cried out, Let no gates opened be;
If he come here, he'll surely cuckold me;
To which the Queen reply'd, with sighs and groans,
No fear, my leidge, for he hes bruised his stones.

Anonymous lines on the death of the first Duke of Argyll, 1703

Then up wi' Geordie, kirn-milk Geordie,
Up wi' Geordie high in a tow.
At the last kick of a foreign foot,
We'se a' be ranting roaring fou.

Anonymous, Kirn-milk Geordie, *Jacobite song against George I (1715)*

Napoleon was an emperor,
He ruled by land and sea;
He was king of France and Germany,
But he ne'er ruled Polmadie.

Anonymous, Johnnie Lad

Andrew Fletcher of Saltoun was notoriously short-tempered. Unable to stand his master's rages, his butler gave notice.
'I cannot bear your temper, sir,' he said.
'Come now,' said Fletcher. 'It's no sooner on than it's off again.'

'Na, sir, it's no sooner off than it's on again.'

Traditional

MacDonald of Keppoch was out with his men one snowy
winter day, tracking down a party from a neighbouring clan
who had raided Keppoch's barnyard for food. As it grew
dark, they resolved to camp for the night rather than return
home. The chief, looking around, asked one of his men to
roll up a big ball of snow, so that he might have something
to rest his head on. The clansmen, hearing this, shook their
heads and muttered to one another: 'How will we ever have
the victory in it when our chief is grown so effeminate he
needs a pillow at night.'

Traditional

O Lord, keep my body frae the doctors, my purse frae the
lawyers, my soul frae the deevil, and my dochters frae the
Laird o' the Glen.

*Macma's Prayer, said to be uttered by tenants at Macma,
Annandale*

Up amid the swells of London,
Mid the pomp of purple sinners,
Where many a kilted thane was undone,
With dice, debauchery, and dinners.

John Stuart Blackie (1809–1895)

may the perfume of her garden
that she tells us is so famous
turn sour as burning flesh
and may her pink and white skin
be stripped from her bones

and spat to herring gulls.
Elizabeth Burns (1957–), The Laird's Wife Visits the Poorhouse

You see yon birkie ca'd a lord,
Wha struts, and stares, and a' that?
Though hundreds worship at his word,
He's but a coof for a' that.

Robert Burns (1759–96), A Man's a Man For a' That

What dost thou in that mansion fair?
Flit, Galloway, and find
Some narrow, dirty, dungeon cave,
The picture of thy mind ...
Bright ran thy line, O Galloway,
Thro' many a far-fam'd sire;
So ran the far-fam'd Roman way,
And ended in a mire!

Robert Burns (1759–1796), Epigrams Against the Earl of Galloway

But gentlemen, an' ladies warst,
Wi' ev'n-down want o' wark are curst.
They loiter, lounging, lank an' lazy;
Tho' deil-haet ails them, yet uneasy ...
Ae night they're mad wi' drink an whuring,
Niest day their life is past enduring.
Robert Burns, The Twa Dogs

The injured Stuart line is gone,
A race outlandish fills their throne;
An idiot race, to honour lost;
Who know them best despise them most.

Robert Burns, Written By Somebody on the Window of an

Inn at Stirling. *Looking up at the then semi-ruinous castle, he inscribed these lines on the House of Hanover.*

... that proud chieftain of the pudding race, the Right Honourable the Earl of Rosebery.

T.W. Crosland, The Unspeakable Scot *(1902)*

From Hell he came in his beginning: his origin makes it easier to believe the news, now that his existence is again prosperous among the hot ash showers of the Devil.

Fionnlagh Ruadh, Red Finlay (16th century), on the death of Allan, Chief of Clanranald (from Gaelic)

Mention not the manly vigour of the man who went in to his mother and to his sister.

Fionnlagh Ruadh, on Allan, chief of Clanranald (from Gaelic)

The Duke then said he would like to hear the Gaelic talked in its purity by two natives of the Highlands. He had a Highland piper attached to his establishment whom he would call up if the Doctor would kindly enter into conversation with him. Dr McLeod said he would be delighted to do so; so the piper was summoned and duly appeared. 'This is Dr McLeod,' said the Duke. 'Ah, yes! your Grace, a' the Hielands ken Dr McLeod.' Taking the initiative, and addressing the piper in Gaelic, the Doctor said, 'Donald, he seems a decent sort of man this master of yours?' Replying in the same language Donald rejoined, 'Hoot aye, man, Doctor! but he's a great fool for a' that!'

Told of Dr Norman McLeod, and the Duke of Sussex, in John Gillespie, The Humours of Scottish Life *(1904)*

Sir Walter Scott was attending the funeral of the Earl of Buchan, the somewhat eccentric nobleman who had the Wallace Monument erected near Dryburgh. The coffin was brought into the chapel head first instead of feet first, and one mourner remarked, 'We have brought the Earl's head in the wrong way.'

Scott replied, 'Never mind, my friends. His Lordship's head was turned when he was alive. It's not worth our while to shift it now.'

Apocryphal tale, from Gordon Irving, The Wit of the Scots *(1969)*

Derby is a very weak-minded fellow I am afraid, and, like the feather pillow, bears the marks of the last person who has sat on him. I hear he is called in London 'genial Judas'!

Earl Haig (1861–1928), letter to his wife, on the Earl of Derby

... the experience of a laird of ancient title who had it pointed out to him that his gamekeeper resembled him so closely they might almost be brothers. Intrigued, he summoned the man and asked him if his mother had ever been in service at the Big House.

'No, my lord,' said the gamekeeper, 'but my father was your mother's butler for a while.'

Cliff Hanley (1922–1999), The Scots

Born into the ranks of the working class, the new King's most likely fate would have been that of a street-corner loafer.

James Keir Hardie (1856–1915), on King George V, 1910

Generation after generation, these few families of tax-gatherers have sucked the life-blood of our nation; in their prides and lusts they have sent us to war, family against family, class against class, race against race; that they might live in idleness and luxury, the labouring mass has sweated and starved; they have pruned the creeds of our Church and stolen its revenues; their mailed fists have crushed the newer thought, and their vanities the arts.

Tom Johnston (1881–1965), Our Scots Noble Families

Show the people that our Old Nobility is not noble, that its lands are stolen lands – stolen either by force or fraud, show people that their title-deeds are rapine, murder, massacre, cheating, or court harlotry . . . shatter the Romance that keeps the nation numb and spellbound while privilege picks its pockets.

Tom Johnston, Our Scots Noble Families

maid Regent in the year of God 1554; and a croune putt upone hir head, als seimlye a sight (yf men had eis) as to putt a saddil upon the back of ane unrewly kow.

John Knox (c. 1507–1572), History of the Reformation in Scotland, *on Mary of Guise, Regent 1554–1560*

. . . greater abomination was never in the nature of any woman than it is in her.

John Knox, History of the Reformation in Scotland, *on Mary, Queen of Scots*

We call hir nott a hoore . . . but sche was brought up in the company of hooremongaris (yea, of such as no more regarded incest, than honest men regard the company of their lauchfull wyeffis) . . . what sche was and is, her self best knowis, and God (we doubt nott) will farther declair.

John Knox, History of the Reformation in Scotland, *on Mary, Queen of Scots*

Our gentyl men are all degenerate;
Liberalitie and Lawtie, both, are loste;
And Cowardice with lords is laureate;
And knichtlie curage turnit in brag and boast.

Sir David Lindsay (c. 1490–1555), Dreme of the Realme of Scotland

. . . lyke ane boisteous bull, ye run and ryde
Ryatouslie lyke ane rubiatoure
Ay fukkand lyke ane furious fornicatour.

Sir David Lindsay, Answer to the King's Flyting, *to King James V (the king's lines to Lindsay have been lost)*

Let Mitchell glorify God in the Grassmarket.

John Maitland, Duke of Lauderdale (1616–82), spoken of James Mitchell, tried in 1678 for the attempted assassination of Archbishop Sharp, which he had done 'for the glory of God'. The Grassmarket was the place of public execution in Edinburgh.

The daughter of a base and brainless breed
Is given what countless better women sorely need . . .
Rope in the shameless hussy, let her be
Directed to factory work or domestic service.
Along with all the other drones and spivs.

Hugh MacDiarmid (C.M. Grieve, 1892–1978), Royal Wedding Gifts, *on public gifts to Princess Elizabeth, 1947*

Henry VIII approached as nearly to the ideal standard of perfect wickedness as the infirmities of human nature will allow.

Sir James Mackintosh (1765–1832), History of England

Although Dunvegan nearly burned down
There was no 'nearly' in the burning of the houses
That MacLeod burned to keep Dunvegan
In grandeur on its rocks.

Sorley MacLean (1911–96), Satire 1: The Castle on Fire *(from Gaelic)*

Mak' your lick-fud bailie core
Fa' down behint him – not afore,
His great posteriors to adore,
Sawney, now the king's come.

Alexander Rodger (1784–1846), Sawney, Now the King's Come, *burlesque of Sir Walter Scott's* Carle, Now the King's Come, *on the occasion of King George IV's visit to Edinburgh in 1822*

We know that the organised workers of the country are our friends. As for the rest, they don't matter a tinker's cuss.

Emmanuel Shinwell (1884–1986), Speech to the Electrical Trades Union Conference, 1947

There goes a carriage with a 'B' outside and a wasp within.

Sydney Smith (1771–1845) on Lord Brougham's monogrammed carriage

The wisest fool in Christendom

Duc de Sully (1559–1641), attributed comment on King

James VI (also ascribed to King Henri IV of France)

One need not dwell on the character of the reigning house, which, brought ignobly to the throne, has been consistently ignoble from the first until the accession of her present Most Gracious Majesty.

James Thomson ('B.V.', 1834–1882), Cope's Tobacco Plant, *1876*

The Queen came by, she looked so sour you could have hung a jug on her mouth.

Christian Watt (1833–1923), The Christian Watt Papers, *on Queen Victoria*

SCHOOLS AND UNIVERSITIES

Mr Rhind is very kind,
He goes to Kirk on Sunday.
He prays to God to give him strength
To skelp the bairns on Monday.

Traditional

Spanner, screwer, lever.

Unofficial motto ascribed to the Royal College of Science & Technology, Glasgow; now the University of Strathclyde

A set o' dull, conceited hashes
confude their brains in college-classes,
They gang in stirks, and come out asses,
Plain truth to speak.

Robert Burns (1759–1796), Epistle to J. Lapraik

A kep and goun –what dae they maitter?
A kep and bells wad suit him better.

Robert Garioch (Robert Garioch Sutherland, 1909–1981),
Garioch's response Til George Buchanan

Professor Blackie of Edinburgh University had to absent
himself from his Greek lectures one day. He wrote on the
blackboard in his lecture-room: 'Professor Blackie regrets
that he cannot meet his classes on Thursday.' A waggish
student rubbed out the 'c' of classes. Blackie, happening to
notice this, also rubbed out the 'l'.

John Gillespie, The Humours of Scottish Life *(1904)*

You could go tae University?
– Whit fir?
Geoff had to think for a while. He had recently graduated
with a degree in English Literature and was on the dole. So
were most of his fellow-graduates. –
It's a good social life, he said.

Irvine Welsh (1957–), Trainspotting

SCOTLAND, AS SEEN BY OTHERS

Some are of Opinion, that, when the Devil showed our
Saviour the Kingdoms of the Earth, he laid his thumb upon
Scotland, and that for a twofold reason: *First,* Because it
was not like to be any Temptation, *Next,* Being Part of his
Mother's Jointure, he could not dispose of it during her Life.

Anonymous, Scotland Observed, *(1701)*

I wondered not, when I was told
The venal Scot his country sold,

I rather very much admire
How he could ever find a buyer.

Anonymous, from Nicholson, Select Collection of Poems, *1780*

A man does well to rid himself of a turd.

King Edward I of England (1239–1307), on leaving Scotland after the Battle of Falkirk, 1298

I look upon Scotland as part of the British Empire, as it were, and when I was a kid I used to look at all the pink on the map and say, 'Isn't that marvellous! We own all that.'

Jimmy Hill, English football commentator, quoted in Roddy Forsyth, The Only Game *(1990)*

Dr Johnson: Sir, it is a very vile country.
Mr S—— : Well, Sir, God made it.
Dr Johnson: Certainly He did, but we must remember He made it for Scotchmen; and comparisons are odious, Mr S——, but God made Hell.

Samuel Johnson (1709–1784), recorded in James Boswell (1740–1795), The Life of Samuel Johnson LLD

. . . the noblest prospect which a Scotchman ever sees, is the high road that leads him to England.

Samuel Johnson

Scotland . . . whose wrinkled surface derives its original from the chaos . . . The country is full of lakes and loughs, and they well stockt with islands, so that a map thereof, looks like a pillory coat bespattered all over with dirt and rotten eggs.

Thomas Kirke, A Modern Account of Scotland by an English Gentleman *(1679)*

This ambassador of the paipis . . . thocht it ane great mervell
that sic ane thing suld be in Scotland considerand that it was
bot the erse of the warld . . .

Robert Lindsay of Pitscottie (c. 1532–80), The Historie and
Cronicles of Scotland, *on the papal ambassador's reaction
to the entertainment laid on by the Earl of Atholl for King
James V in 1531*

That garret of the earth – the knuckle-end of England – that
land of Calvin, oat-cakes and sulphur

Sydney Smith (1771–1845), quoted in Lady Holland, A
Memoir of the Rev. Sydney Smith

The air might be wholesome but for the stinking people that
inhabit it; the ground might be fruitful had they the wit to
manure it.

Sir Anthony Weldon, A Perfect Description of the People
and Country of Scotland *(1617)*

SCOTS, AS SEEN BY OTHERS

God send the land deliverance
Frae every reiving, riding Scot;
We'll sune hae neither cow nor ewe,
We'll sune hae neither staig nor stot.

Anonymous, The Death of Parcy Reed

. . . there are no finer Gentlemen in the World, than that
Nation can justly boast of; but then they are such as have
travelled, and are indebted to other Countries for those
Accomplishments that render them so esteemed, their own
affording only Pedantry, Poverty, Brutality, and Hypocrisy.

Anonymous, Scotland Characterised, *1701*

See how they press to cross the Tweed,
And strain their limbs with eager speed!
While Scotland from her fertile shore
Cries, On my sons, return no more.
Hither they haste with willing mind,
Nor cast one longing look behind.

Anonymous English verse, 18th century

What is a Scot but an uninspired Irishman?

Anonymous remark noted in Forsyth Hardy, John Grier-son's Scotland *(1979)*

I have been greatly disgusted with the appearance of the brave Highlanders. They strike me as stupid, dirty, ignorant and barbarous. Their mode of life is not different from that of African negroes. Their huts are floorless except for earth, and they all live together in them like pigs; there are no chimneys, hardly any windows; no conveniences of life of any sort.

Henry Adams, American visitor, in a letter to C.F. Adams, 1863

... the Scots are not industrious ... They spend all their time in wars, and when there is no war they fight with one another.

Don Pedro de Ayala, Spanish Ambassador to King James IV, official report, July 1498

... of the Scots he said that they were ugly but good-natured ... 'They are kind, but so boring that the Lord preserve them.'

T. Ratcliffe Barnet, on Frederic Chopin's stay in Scotland, Scottish Pilgrimage in the Land of Lost Content *(1949)*

The devellysche dysposicion of a Scottis man, not to love nor favour an Englis man. . . Trust yow no Skott.

Andrew Boorde, English agent, letter to Thomas Cromwell, 1536

Then thousand schemes of petulance and pride
Despatch her scheming children far and wide:
Some east. some west, some everywhere but north,
In quest of lawless gain they issue forth.

Lord Byron (1788–1824), The Curse of Minerva

Had *Cain* been Scot, God would have chang'd his doom;
Not forc'd him wander, but confin'd him home.

J. Cleveland, Poems, *1647*

Hadrian had the excellent sense to build a wall for the purpose of keeping the Scotch out of England.

T.W. Crosland, The Unspeakable Scot *(1902)*

A Scotchman does certainly make one feel that underneath his greasy and obviously imperfect civilisation the hairy simian sits and gibbers.

T.W. Crosland, The Unspeakable Scot

IF WITHOUT SERIOUS INCONVENIENCE TO YOUR-
SELF YOU CAN MANAGE TO REMAIN AT HOME,
PLEASE DO.

T.W. Crosland, The Unspeakable Scot, *Item 10 of advice to young Scots planning a career in England*

They are all gentlemen and insolent to the last degree. But certainly the absurdity is ridiculous to see a man in his mountain habit, armed with a broad sword, target, pistol or perhaps two, in his girdle a dagger, and a staff, walking down the street as upright and haughty as if he were a lord . . . and withal driving a cow.

Daniel Defoe (1660–1731), Letters, quoted in Maurice Lindsay, The Discovery of Scotland *(1964)*

A hardened, refractory people.

Daniel Defoe, Letters, on the Scots

Treacherous Scotland, to no interest true.

John Dryden (1631–1700)

subsidy junkies

The London Evening Standard, *1987, quoted in Maurice Smith,* Paper Lions: the Scottish Press and National Identity *(1994)*

If the Scots knew enough to go indoors when it rained, they would never get any exercise.

Simeon Ford (1855–1933), American visitor, My Trip to Scotland

The foul hordes of Scots and Picts like dark throngs of worms . . . a set of bloody freebooters, with more hair on their thievish faces than clothes to cover their nakedness.

Gildas (c. 493–570), De Excidio et Conquestu Britanniae, *on the Picts, from Latin*

Among ourselves, the Scotch, as a nation, are particularly disagreeable. They hate every appearance of comfort themselves and refuse it to others. Their climate, their religion and their habits are equally averse to pleasure.

Their manners are either distinguished by a fawning sycophance (to gain their own ends, and conceal their natural defects), that makes one sick; or by a morose, unbending callousness, that makes one shudder.

William Hazlitt (1778–1839), Essays

... we know they can remedy their poverty when they set about it. No-one is sorry for them.

William Hazlitt, Essays

... when they smile, I feel an involuntary emotion to guard myself against mischief.

'Junius', Letters *(1770)*

There was very little amusement in the room but a Scotchman to hate ... At Taylor's, too, there was a Scotchman – not quite so bad for he was as clean as he could get himself.

John Keats (1795–1821), Letters

The people are proud, arrogant, vain-glorious boasters, bloody, barbarous and inhuman butchers. Couzenage and theft is in perfection among them, and they are perfect English haters, they show their pride in exalting themselves, and depressing their neighbours.

Thomas Kirke, A Modern Account of Scotland by an English Gentleman *(1679)*

The tediousness of these people is certainly provoking. I wonder if they ever tire one another! In my early life I had a passionate fondness for the poetry of Burns. I have sometimes foolishly hoped to ingratiate myself with his

countrymen by expressing it. But I have always found that a
true Scot resents your admiration of his compatriot, even
more than he would your contempt of him. The latter he
imputes to your 'imperfect acquaintance with many of the
words which he uses;' and the same objection makes it a
presumption in you to suppose that you can admire him.

Charles Lamb (1775–1834), An Imperfect Acquaintance, *in*
Essays of Elia

Among the Highlanders generally, to rob was thought at
least as honourable an employment as to cultivate the soil.

Lord Macaulay (1800–1859), History of England

I am glad to see you make a point of calling them
'Scotchmen' not 'Scotsmen' as they like to be called. I find
this a good easy way of annoying them.

*George Orwell (Eric Blair, 1903–1950), Letter to Anthony
Powell, 1936, quoted in Christopher Harvie,* Travelling
Scot *(1999)*

Athenians, indeed! where is your theatre? who among you
has written a comedy? where is your Attic salt? which of
you can tell who was Jupiter's great-grandfather? . . . you
know nothing that the Athenians thought worth knowing,
and dare not show your faces before the civilised world in
the practice of any one art in which they were excellent.

*Thomas Love Peacock (1785–1866), on the pretensions of
Edinburgh as the 'Athens of the North', in* Crotchet Castle
(1831)

It is said that a Scotchman returning home, after some
years' residence in England, being asked what he thought of
the English, answered: 'They hanna ower muckle sense, but

they are an unco braw people to live amang;' which would
be a very good story, if it were not rendered apocryphal, by
the incredible circumstance of the Scotchman going back.

Thomas Love Peacock, Crotchet Castle

Such Mediocrity was ne'er on view,
Bolster'd by tireless Scottish Ballyhoo –
Nay! In two qualities they stand supreme;
Their self-advertisement and their self-esteem.

Anthony Powell (fl. 18th century), Caledonia

It requires a surgical operation to get a joke well into a
Scotch understanding. Their only idea of wit, or rather that
inferior variety of this electric talent which prevails
occasionally in the north, and which, under the name of
wut, is so infinitely distressing to people of good taste, is
laughing immoderately at stated intervals.

Sydney Smith (1771–1845), quoted in Lady Holland,
Memorial of the Rev. Sydney Smith *(1855)*

There are some people who think they sufficiently acquit
themselves, and entertain their company, with relating facts
of no consequence, but at all out of the road of such
common incidents as happen every day; and this I have
observed more frequently among the Scots than any other
nation.

Jonathan Swift (1667–1745), Hints Towards an Essay on
Conversation

Their beasts be generally small, women only excepted, of
which sort there are none greater in the whole world ...
To be chained in marriage with one of them, were to be tied
to a dead carcass, and cast into a stinking ditch; formosity

and a dainty face are things they dream not of.

Sir Anthony Weldon, A Perfect Description of the People and Country of Scotland *(1617)*

It is never difficult to distinguish between a Scotsman with a grievance and a ray of sunshine.

P.G. Wodehouse (1881–1975), quoted in Richard Usborne, Wodehouse at Work *(1961)*

SPORTS

Brissit brawnis and broken banis,
Stride, discord, and waistie wanis;
Crukit in eild, syne halt withal –
Thir are the bewties of the fute-ball.

Anonymous, The Bewties of the Fute-Ball

Th'athletic fool to whom what Heav'n denied
Of soul is well compensated in limbs

John Armstrong (c. 1709–1779), The Art of Preserving Health

Tully produced a complimentary admission ticket from the waistband of his playing shorts during a game in which he was getting the better of his immediate opponent, the fearsome full-back Don Emery. He handed it to Emery, with the observation, 'Here, would you not be better watching from the stand?'

Peter Burns and Pat Woods, Oh, Hampden in the Sun *(1997), on Charlie Tully, Celtic star of the late 1940s*

In Glasgow, half the fans hate you and the other half think
they own you.

Tommy Burns (1956–), quoted in Kenny MacDonald,
Scottish Football Quotations *(1994)*

I support Partick Thistle. They'll be in Europe next year. If
there's a war on.

Billy Connolly (1942–), quoted in D. Campbell, Billy
Connolly: The Authorised Version *(1976)*

My son was born to play for Scotland. He has all the
qualities, a massive ego, a criminal record, an appalling
drink problem. And he's not very good at football.

*'Mrs Alice Cosgrove', quoted on the back cover of Stuart
Cosgrove,* Hampden Babylon *(1991)*

He says, 'Who are you?' I says, 'Albion Rovers.' He says,
'Never heard of them.' I said, 'You ignorant bugger.' But it
was a natural thing. I mean, it wisnae him alone – there
were other people who'd never heard of Albion Rovers.

*Tom Fagan of Albion Rovers, on a FIFA meeting, 1985,
quoted in K. Macdonald,* Scottish Football Quotations *(1994)*

They christened their game golf because they were Scottish
and revelled in meaningless Celtic noises in the back of the
throat.

Stephen Fry (1957–), Paperweight

. . . the Partick Thistle supporters' anthem goes like this:
'We hate Roman Catholics,
We hate Protestants too,
We hate Jews and Muslims:

Partick Thistle we love you . . . '

Alasdair Gray (1934–), The Trendelenburg Position, in S. Maguire and D. Jackson Young, Hoots (1967)

There was a woman there with the blue eye-shadow and the red lipstick and I was walking off and she called me a big dirty Fenian bastard. I turned and said, 'Oh, come on,' and she said, 'Nothing personal, I know your Auntie Annie.'

Tony Higgins, striker for Hibernian FC, in in the BBC TV documentary, It's Only a Game (1985)

Eck: . . . This is where I come to do what the Scots are best at.'
Willie: Shinty?
Eck: Moping.

John McKay, Dead Dad Dog (1988)

Rabid and bigoted partisanship is an exceedingly mild term to apply to their ferocious ebulations. Were they of the working class there might be a little excuse for them, but the most of them at any rate are dressed like gentlemen. I am afraid the resemblance ends there. A worse exhibition than these gents favoured us with has not been given in Scotland. It was worthy of a band of drunken cannibals.

John H. MacLauchlin in the Glasgow Examiner, 1896, on Queen's Park supporters, the 'Hampdenites'

Slim Jim had everything required of a great Scottish footballer. Outrageously skilled, totally irresponsible, supremely arrogant and thick as mince.

Alastair McSporran on the Rangers player Jim Baxter, in the fanzine The Absolute Game (1990)

Three things are thrown away on a bowling green, namely, time, money, and oaths.

Sir Walter Scott (1771–1832), The Fortunes of Nigel

After a lengthy goal famine had struck Scotland, it was rumoured that on one foreign trip, striker Gordon Durie couldn't find his way into the team hotel. Someone had painted goalposts over the door.

Tom Shields, Tom Shields Too *(1993)*

As a young Rangers player, Alex Ferguson . . . was unhappy at being left out of the first team. He stormed into the office of legendary manager Scott Symon. 'Why have I been in the second team for three weeks?' he asked. The magisterial Mr Symon replied, 'Because we don't have a third team.'

Tom Shields, Tom Shields Too

Shankly, who once played for a very minor Scottish team called Glenbuck Cherrypickers, is also alleged to have put his head round the door of the visitors' dressing room after a goalless game and announced, 'The better team drew.'

W. Gordon Smith, This Is My Country *(1976), on Bill Shankly, football manager (1914–1981)*

We do have the greatest fans in the world but I've never seen a fan score a goal.

Jock Stein (1922–1985), quoted in A. Cran and J. Robertson, A Dictionary of Scottish Quotations *(1996)*

People say that the Souness revolution was responsible for the rise in Rangers support but I think it's more to do with the Government Care in the Community policies, which threw these unfortunates onto the streets.

Irvine Welsh (1957–), interviewed on ErinWeb, 1997

TRADITIONS AND FESTIVITIES

Edinburgh Festival audiences applaud everything with equal indiscrimination.

Sir Thomas Beecham (1879–1961)

I deeply regret that we have not finished yet.

Sir Thomas Beecham, to an Usher Hall audience that clapped prematurely (1956)

All that is desired is (1) to get some useful publicity; (2) make money; and (3) jack up a little the general illusion that the Scots are really a cultured people with an interest in the arts. In short, it is just another lousy racket.

Hugh MacDiarmid (C.M. Grieve 1892–1978), The Company I've Kept, *on the plan for the Edinburgh Festival*

Sin a' oor wit is in oor wame,
Wha'll flyte us for a lack o' lair;
Oor guts maun glorify your name
Sin a' oor wit is in oor wame.

William Soutar (1898–1943), From Any Burns Club to Scotland, *on once-a-year Burnsians*

. . . the residents of the southern suburbs of Marchmont and Morningside used to pull down their front window blinds on the 11th of August, for a fortnight, and retire to the back

rooms – to give the impression that they had departed North
for the grouse-shooting.

Nigel Tranter (1909–2000)

TRAVEL AND TRANSPORT

I'm now arriv'd – thanks to the gods!
Thro' pathways rough and muddy:
A certain sign that makin' roads
Is no this people's study.
Altho' I'm not wi' Scripture cram'd,
I'm sure the Bible says
That heedless sinners shall be damn'd
Unless they mend their ways.

Robert Burns (1759–1796), Epigram on Rough Roads

. . . the *Suilven* is a floating extension of Ullapool's chip-
strewn littoral.

Derek Cooper (1925–), The Road to Mingulay, *on a
Hebridean car ferry*

A worthy countryman who had come from the north-east
side of the kingdom by train to Cowlairs, was told that the
next stoppage would be Glasgow. He at once began to get
all his little packages ready, and remarked to a fellow-
passenger, 'I'm sailin' for China this week, but I'm thinkin'
I'm by the warst o' the journey noo.'

Sir Archibald Geikie (1835–1924), Scottish Reminiscences. *A jibe at the Caledonian Railway, but the same
story is told about all the Scottish railway companies.*

There was one the other day when the train was running along at its steady three miles an hour, and he tried to be funny. He said, 'I say, guard,' Fyffe enjoyed imitating the English and American accents – 'could I get out to pick a few flowers on the embankment while the train is in motion?' Oh, I was leerie for him. I said, 'If ye look oot, ye'll see there's nae flooers on this embankment.' 'Oh, that's all right,' said he, 'I've brought a packet of seeds.'

Albert D. Mackie, The Scottish Comedians *(1973), on Will Fyffe's impersonation of a Highland Railway guard*

The Day of Judgement is at hand when the MacBrayne steamer will be on time.

Ian Crichton Smith (1928–1998), Thoughts of Murdo

WARFARE

Ladies from Hell.

German description of kilted Scottish troops, World War I

Poison dwarfs.

German description of the Highland Light Infantry, in the post-World War II Occupation of West Germany

They sent me word that I was like the first puff of a haggis, hottest at the first.

Sir Robert Carey, Warden of the March, of a message from the Armstrongs in 1601, quoted in George Macdonald Fraser, The Steel Bonnets *(1971)*

I have seen better-dressed and more capable dummies than you outside cinemas.

Said to have been shouted on a megaphone by Captain Swanson of the St Ola *to the commander of Scrabster harbour in World War II, recorded in Jo Grimond (1913–93),* Memoirs

There's some that we wan,
Some say that they wan,
Some say that nane wan at a', man;
But o' ae thing I'm sure,
That at Sherrifmuir,
A battle there was that I saw, man.
And we ran, and they ran,
And they ran, and we ran,
And they ran and we ran awa', man.

Murdoch MacLennan (fl. early 18th century), Sheriffmuir

Hey! Johnnie Cope, are ye walkin' yet?
Or are your drums a-beating yet?
If ye were walking I wad wait
To gang to the coals in the morning!

Adam Skirving (1719–1803), Johnnie Cope

WIVES AND HUSBANDS

'Ye've gey little to complain o', man. Ye should be thankful ye're no married tae her.'

Lord Braxfield (1722–1799) to his butler, who complained about Lady Braxfield's manner

'Ye damned stupid bitch . . . I beg your pardon, mem. I took ye for my wife.'

Lord Braxfield, to his partner at whist

Yestreen I had a pint o' wine,
A place where body saw na;
Yestreen lay on this breast o' mine,
The gowden locks of Anna . . .
The Kirk and State may join and tell,
To do sic things I mauna:
The Kirk and State may gae to hell,
And I'll gae to my Anna.

Robert Burns (1759–1796), The Gowden Locks of Anna.
Anna Park, a Dumfries barmaid, was mother of his last child.

She has an e'e, she has but ane,
The cat has twa the very colour;
Five rusty teeth, forbye a stump,
A clapper tongue wad deave a miller;
A whiskin beard about her mou',
Her nose and chin they threaten ither;
Sic a wife as Willie had,
I wad na gie a button for her.

Robert Burns, Willie Wastle

She tauld thee weel thou wast a skellum,
A blethering, blustering, drunken blellum

Robert Burns, Tam o' Shanter

. . . a Highland woman, who, begging a charity of a
Lowland laird's lady, was asked several questions, and,
among the rest, how many husbands she had had? To which
she answered, three. And being further questioned, if her

husbands had been kind to her, she said the first two were
honest men, and very careful of their family, for they both
'died for the law' – that is, were hanged for theft. 'Well, but
as to the last?' 'Hout!' says she, 'a fulthy peast! He dy'd at
hame, lik an auld dug, on a puckle o' strae.'

Edmund Burt (c. 1695–1755), Letters from a Gentleman in
the North of Scotland *(1726–37)*

Ay, when that caribald carl wald climb on my wame,
Then am I dangerus and dain and dour of my will;
Yet let I never that larbar my leggis gae between,
To fyle my flesh, na fumyll me, without a fee great.

William Dunbar (c. 1460–c. 1520), The Tretis of the Twa
Mariit Wemen and the Wedo

The indignant husband explained the reason for his wrath:
had he not good cause for stabbing a wife who was unfaithful to him? If he expected the cummers of Aberlady to
sympathise, and denounce the erring woman, he got a drop,
for one of them stepped forward and retorted, 'Losh, if that
be the trouble, you might as well stick us a' in Aberlady.'

Augustus Muir, Heather Track and High Road *(1944)*

WOMEN

They say in Fife
That next to nae wife,
The best thing is a gude wife.

Traditional

Though all the wood under heaven that grows

Were crafty pennis convenient for to write . . .
All the men were writtaris that ever took life
Could not write the false dissaitful despite
And wicketness contenit in a wife.

Anonymous, 16th century

Here lyes a Maid not full sixteen,
Who was a servant to the Queen.
More men than years she had upon her,
But still she was a Maid of Honour.

Anonymous, 17th century, On a Maid of Honour

Here lyes enshrin'd in this foul lining
The mother of Jock and Willie Bining,
Who lived a miser, died ane witch,
And now to hell they hurl'd the bitch . . .
Her wynding sheet is ane old shirt,
Her funerall oyls are piss and dirt,
Her coffin is of ane old girnell,
Earth keeps the shell, the deil the kirnell.

*Anonymous, 17th century, perhaps aimed at William
Binning, Provost of Edinburgh in 1676 (from James
Maidment's* Scottish Pasquils, *1868)*

She's fair and fause that causes my smart.

Robert Burns (1759–1796), She's Fair and Fause

The Almighty made all things very good without doubt, but
he left some mighty queer kinks in woman. But then the
whole affair of her creation was an afterthought.

S.R. Crockett (1859–1914)

Until a woman is free to be as incompetent as the average male then she never will be completely equal.

Rosanna Cunningham MP, quoted in The Independent, *(May 2, 1995), from A. Cran and J. Robertson,* Dictionary of Scottish Quotations *(1996)*

She haunts the sculleries and parlours of Scotland's social history like an irreversible curse. She patrols our psyche like a bossy traffic warden . . . She is Black Agnes of the but-and-ben, scolding her men-folk, stiffening their backbone, sacrificing herself and her daughters on the altar of their incompetence.

Julie Davidson, on the Scottish mother-figure as personified by 'Ma Broon', The Scotsman, *19 February 1979*

Nature, I say, doth paynt them further to be weak, fraile, impacient, feble, and foolish; and experience hath declared them to be unconstant, variable, cruell, and lacking the spirit of counsel and regiment.

John Knox (c. 1505–1572), The First Blast of the Trumpet Against the Monstrous Regiment of Women

To promote a Woman to beare rule, superioritie, dominion or empire above any Realme, Nation or Citie, is repugnant to Nature; contumelie to God, a thing most contrary to his revealed will and approvedordinance, and finallie it is the subversion of good Order, of all equitie and justice.

John Knox, The First Blast of the Trumpet Against the Monstrous Regiment of Women

The island women, on the whole, are plain; and many of them are exceedingly so. This applies to the young, as well as to the middle-aged and elderly.

Alasdair Alpin MacGregor, The Western Isles *(1949)*

What is yon crew in the black ship, pulling her among the waves? A crew without fellowship, without sense, a disorderly-minded band of women.

Let us leave on the stormy stream the the evil, leaky ship, and its load of noxious women, in the salt brine, without psalm or sea-creed.

The McIntyre Bard, 14th-15th century, from W.J. Watson, Scottish Verse from the Book of the Dean of Lismore *(1937), from Gaelic*

She's a classy girl, though, at least all her tattoos are spelt right.

Chic Murray (1919–1985), The Chic Murray Bumper Book *(1990)*

. . . that mim-moothed snivellin' fule,
A fushionless woman.

Dorothy Margaret Paulin (b.1904), Said the Spaewife

. . . the best opposite sex that men have got.

Jimmy Reid (1932–), The Glasgow Herald, *March 1981*

They would have all men bound and thrall
To them, and they for to be free.

Alexander Scott (c. 1520–c. 1590), Of Womankind

Woman's faith and woman's trust:
Write the characters in dust.

Sir Walter Scott (1771–1832), The Betrothed

He worried about her, however, thinking that anyone who would sleep with him would sleep with anybody.

Irvine Welsh (1957–), Trainspotting

GREAT INSULTERS

Thomas Carlyle

Thomas Carlyle (1795–1881) was one of the great men of the Victorian era. Historian, novelist, philosopher, he had a gift for expressing his views in a trenchant and original way. His writing style, heavily influenced by his reading of German, is a demanding one for the modern reader, but within his convoluted prose there are hundreds of crisp and strongly-worded judgements. Carlyle did not suffer fools gladly – he did not suffer them at all. He was quite capable of writing off the entire English nation – he lived most of his adult life in London – as 'mostly fools'. His enmity with Swinburne arose from his dislike of Swinburne's writing, hence the comment that Swinburne was 'standing in a cess-pool, and adding to it (often wrongly given as 'sitting in a sewer'). Swinburne himself began as an admirer of Carlyle. But by the time of Carlyle's death, Swinburne was referring to him as 'this dead snake'. Some of Carlyle's prejudices were ugly ones; he referred to the humanitarian reformer William Wilberforce as 'the famous Nigger-Philanthropist, Drawing-room Christian, and busy man and Politician'. His references to Disraeli reveal a streak of anti-semitism. But at least he was his own man, with little respect for public opinion: 'The public is an old woman. Let her maunder and mumble'; or for the aristocracy and royalty. Of the 'sun-king' Louis XIV he wrote: 'Strip your Louis XIV of his king gear and there is left nothing but a poor forked radish with a head fantastically carved.'

Carlyle's presence was strong enough to deliver an insult without a word being said – see the Manners section. Henry James called Carlyle 'an old sausage, fizzing and sputtering in its own grease'.

A GREAT INSULTER.
THOMAS CARLYLE
1795 – 1881.

The Flyters

William Dunbar, who lived approximately between 1460 and 1520, was court poet to King James IV, and a keen practitioner of the poetic art of 'flyting', a relic perhaps of the formal disputations that were common in medieval scholarship. A flyting was a dialogue between two poets in which each set out to vaunt his own abilities and decry those of his rival. There was a real purpose behind them – the poet who appeared to have won the verbal joust would be rewarded with the royal favour and royal gold: the loser would have his status reduced – at least until next time. In this way, among others, the 15th century Scottish court spent the long winter evenings. One of the flytings that has been recorded is that between Dunbar and his fellow-poet, Walter Kennedy. Writing in Scots, both made full use of that language's alliterative expressiveness:

Says Kennedy:
Ignorant elf, aip, owll irregular,
Skaldit skaitbird, and common shamelar;
Wan-fukkit funling, that natour maid ane yrle,
Baith Iohine the Ros and thow sall squeill and skirle,
And evir I heir ocht of your making mair.

Says Dunbar, picking on Kennedy's provincial Ayrshire Gaelic background:
Iersche brybour bard, vyle beggar with thy brattis
Cuntbittin crawdoun Kennedy, coward of kynd . . .
They trechour tung has tane ane heland strynd –
Ane lawland ers wald make a bettir noyis.
King James V was not above such verbal tilts himself. He wrote a flyting against Sir David Lindsay, poet and member of the court circle. Lindsay responded with no holds barred (see Royalty section). In another poem, he bemoans the fact that the king has not made him a lord – perhaps the 'aye

GREAT INSULTERS
THE FLYTERS

fukkand' 'rude rubiatoure' had been stung a little too deeply in the flyting.

Robert Burns

Robert Burns (1759–1796) was normally an easy-going and sociable individual. Certainly the man who wrote 'Man to man, the world o'er, shall brothers be for a' that', was anything but a hater of his fellow-men. But Burns was a fiery spirit and his awareness of his own abilities, combined with the patronising attitude of those in better-off circles, often made him resentful. He also detested hypocrisy in all its forms, including the religious hypocrisy common in his day, when the 'unco-guid' often preached one set of behaviour and practised another.

This detestation gave rise to *Holy Willie's Prayer,* one of the most powerful and damning satirical poems ever written. 'Holy Willie' was a real person, William Fisher. History does not record his reaction to the lines that must have made a whole countryside laugh behind its hand whenever he appeared in public:

'O lord! yestreen, thou kens, wi' Meg –
Thy pardon I sincerely beg,
O! may't never be a livin' plague to my dishonour,
An' I'll ne'er lift a lawless leg
Again upon her.'

Towards the end of his short life, Burns was taken up by the well-off Riddell family, who lived near his home. But after some drunken pranks, in which the men of the party pretended to carry out a 'Rape of the Sabine Women' on the ladies, the relationship ended. Burns had behaved no worse than any of the 'gentlemen' present, but he was felt to have gone beyond what his social position allowed. When his apologies were refused, he turned to scorn. A poet's vengeance lasts a long time. If the Riddells are now remembered, it is through lines such as these, *Pinned to Mrs Walter Riddell's Carriage*:

'If you rattle along like your mistress's tongue,
Your speed will outrival the dart;
But a fly for your load, you'll break down on the road,
If your stuff be as rotten's her heart.'

Hugh MacDiarmid

Hugh MacDiarmid (Christopher Murray Grieve, 1892–1978) fought a lifelong battle on behalf of many causes, political, national, literary and linguistic. His early poems in Scots are regarded by many critics as the finest Scottish poetry of the twentieth century. MacDiarmid once compared himself to a volcano, erupting large amounts of rubbish as well as fire: his temper was always on a short fuse and his capacity for scorn was as great as his own self-esteem. The gloomy decade of the 1930s was enlivened, or perhaps further depressed, by a literary feud between MacDiarmid and another poet of great distinction, Edwin Muir, on the capacity of Scotland to sustain a genuine literary culture. MacDiarmid felt that Muir had sold out to the English and let fly at him. Muir was allied with 'a worthless set of people – a historically-doomed class of petit-bourgeois due for speedy liquidation'.

Muir, a milder man, did not resort to abuse, but did pass comment on the Scots writers of his time: 'Men of sorrow, and acquainted with Grieve.'

MacDiarmid's relationship with his home town of Langholm was another storm zone, during his life and after his death. Not ever one to suffer from Scottish mealy-mouthedness, he

A GREAT INSULTER
ROBERT BURNS
1759 – 1796.

had said rude things about the townsfolk and their level of thought. Langholm reciprocated with a refusal to honour its most famous son. But then he had written:

'O arselins wi' them! Whummle them again!
Coup them heels-owre-gowdy in a storm sae gundy
That mony a lang fog-theekit face I ken
'll be sooked richt doon under a cundy
In the High Street.'

Not many of his contemporaries could rival MacDiarmid's relish for combat and the verbal energy at his disposal, but one who hit back with some spirit was Lauchlan Maclean Watt, minister and minor literary figure. Mocked in MacDiarmid's poem *To Circumjack Cencrastus,* he said in a review of the work:

It is not poetry. Here, most frequently, we have neither rhyme nor reason. We have the utterance of much that should never find expression in decent society . . . It sounds like Homer after he had swallowed his false teeth.

A GREAT INSULTER
HUGH MacDIARMID
1892 — 1978.

INDEX OF AUTHORS

Scottish authors are indicated by *

A

Adams, Henry 151
Allan, John R.* 48, 63
Anton, James 40
Arbuthnot, John* 33, 124
Armstrong, John* 157
Arnold, Matthew 79
Askey, Arthur 24
Asquith, H.H. 124
Ayala, Don Pedro de 151
Aytoun, W.E.* 67

B

Bagehot, Walter 101
Baillie, Joanna* 98
Baird, John Logie* 79
Balfour, Arthur James* 2, 124, 125
Bannerman, John* 48
Barnet, T. Ratcliffe* 151
Barrie, Sir J.M.* 5, 36, 40, 72, 98, 133
Bax, Sir Arnold 65
Baxter, Stanley* 24
Beattie, James* 102
Beaverbrook,Lord 102
Beecham, Sir Thomas 161
Bell, Joseph* 5
Bellany, John* 102
Birley, Anthony 134
Black, William* 49
Blackhall, Sheena* 49
Blackie, John Stuart* 140
Blair, Hamish* 114
Blair, Robert* 21
Blair, Tony 124
Blue, Jamie* 102
Bold, Alan* 88
Boorde, Andrew 152
Boswell, James* 21

Boyd, Eddie* 61
Braxfield, Lord* 90, 93, 164
Bridie, J.M.* 37, 76
Brogan, Colm* 125
Brooksbank, Mary* 67
Brougham, Lord* 5, 31
Brown, Gordon* 125
Bruce, Steve* 86
Buchan, Tom* 79, 88
Buckle, Henry Thomas 79
Burnet, Gilbert* 21, 125
Burns, Elizabeth* 140
Burns, Peter* 157
Burns, Robert* 1, 5, 15, 16, 33–36, 41, 63, 66, 75, 76, 79, 81, 94, 97, 103, 114, 125, 141, 147, 162, 165, 167, 175
Burns, Tommy* 158
Burt, Edmund 13, 24, 41, 88, 165
Burton, John Hill* 134
Butler, Samuel 103
Byron, Lord 5, 16, 57, 60, 61, 88, 152

C

Cameron, H.J.* 81
Campbell, Angus* 1
Campbell, Thomas* 66, 72, 126
Carey, Sir Robert 163
Carlyle, Jane Welsh* 25
Carlyle, Thomas* 3, 6, 21, 49, 62, 70, 96, 98, 114, 171
Carswell, Catherine* 99
Carswell, Donald* 6, 50, 72, 81
Carswell, John* 90
Chalmers, Thomas* 81
Chambers, Robert* 81
Charles II, King 82
Chopin, Frederic 25

Christiansen, Rupert 6
Churchill, Charles 25
Churchill, Winston 103, 126
Cleveland, J. 152
Clough, Arthur Hugh 114
Cockburn, Lord* 67, 114, 115
Cocker, W.D.* 41, 71, 82
Colville, Samuel* 6
Connolly, Billy* 26, 62, 89, 158
Connolly, Cyril 103
Cooper, Derek 162
Cosgrove, Stuart* 158
Crockett, S.R.* 167
Crosland, T.W. 6, 14, 126, 142, 152
Crumley, Jim* 115
Cumming, Alan* 118
Cunningham, Allan* 127
Cunningham, Rosanna* 169
Currie, Ken* 3

D
Dalyell, Tam* 127
Dante, Alighieri 101
Davidson, Julie* 169
Defoe, Daniel 152, 153
Devon, Dr James* 97
Dewar, Donald* 26
Dibdin, James C. 26
Dickens, Charles 73
Dodd, Ken 26
Douglas, Archbishop* 16
Douglas, George* 37
Douglas, Norman* 22, 41, 58, 65, 72, 89, 104
Douglas, O.* 99
Douglas, Sheila* 50
Drummond, William* 75
Dryden, John 153
Duffy, Carol Anne* 127
Dunbar, Archbishop* 16
Dunbar, William* 37, 50, 104, 115, 166, 173

E
Edgar, John* 91
Edward I, King of England 149
Elcho, Lord* 104
Erskine, Thomas* 8, 97, 133
Ewing, Winnie* 127

F
Fadiman, C. 129
Fagan, Tom* 158
Fairbairn, Sir Nicholas* 76, 128
Fergusson, Robert* 42, 62
Finlay, Ian Hamilton* 4
Finnie, Mr* 82
Finniston, Sir Monty* 50
Fionnlagh Ruadh* 142
Fleming, Arnold* 134
Fletcher, Andrew* 128
Ford, Robert* 42, 94
Ford, Simeon 153
Fox, Charles James 95
Fraser, G.S.* 64, 115
Fraser, George Macdonald* 50, 68, 101
Fraser, John* 9
Fry, Stephen 158

G
Garioch, Robert* 104, 148
Geddes, Alexander* 22
Geddes, Jenny* 17
Geddes, Sir Patrick* 115
Geikie, Sir Archibald* 162
Gib, Adam* 83
Gibbon, Lewis Grassic* 9, 68, 83, 89, 104, 116
Gildas 153
Gillespie, John* 83, 135, 142, 148
Glass, Jack* 63
Gordon, Joe* 14
Graham, H. Grey* 4, 78
Graham, R.B. Cunninghame* 58, 127
Gray, Alasdair* 50, 99, 158

Gray, Muriel* 74
Greacen, Robert* 17
Grimond, Jo 117, 164
Guedalla, Philip 22
Gunn, George* 60
Gunn, Neil M.* 1

H
Haig, Earl* 143
Hamilton, Iain* 117
Hammerton, J.A. 22
Hancock, Sheila 26
Hanley, Cliff* 51, 117, 143
Hardie, James Keir* 143
Harvie, Christopher* 129
Hay, Ian* 64
Hazlitt, William 154
Henderson, Hamish* 9, 57, 70
Henryson, Robert* 18
Higgins, Tony* 159
Hill, Jimmy 149
Hind, Archie* 37
Hislop, Alexander* 83, 96, 135
Hogg, James* 23, 38, 69
Hopkins, Kenneth 9
Housman, A.E. 10
Hume, David* 22, 84, 105
Hume, Patrick, of Polwarth* 55

I
Irving, Gordon* 105, 143

J
Jackson, Alan* 2, 51, 73, 105
Jacob, Violet* 99
James VI, King* 10, 51, 74, 84
James, Clive 105
Jeffrey, Lord* 10
Johnson, Samuel 23, 105, 149
Johnston, Archibald, of Wariston*
     129
Johnston, Tom* 143, 144
'Junius' 154

K
Kames, Lord* 95
Keats, John 59, 154
Kelman, James* 10, 46, 129
Kelvin, Lord 84
Kennaway, James* 98
Kennedy, Walter* 173
Kesson, Jessie* 99
Kirke, Thomas 149, 154
Knox, John* 144, 169

L
Laing, R.D.* 85
Lamb, Charles 106, 154
Lamont, Norman* 71
Lauderdale, Duke of* 145
Law, T.S.* 74
Lawrence, D.H. 106
Lawrence, T.E. 117
Leland, John* 65
Leyden, John* 91
Lindsay, Sir David* 27, 51, 145
Lindsay, Maurice* 10
Lindsay, Robert, of Pitscottie 150
Linklater, Eric* 38, 52
Lipton, Douglas* 59
Little, Janet* 11
Livingstone, David* 58
Lloyd George, David 128
Loch, James* 52
Lochhead, Liz* 69
Lockhart, George* 106
Lockhart, J.G.* 11

M
Macaulay, Lord 11, 155
MacCodrum, John* 14
McConal, Tyrell* 52
MacDiarmid, Hugh* 11, 12, 18,
     46, 52, 62, 67, 68, 70, 85, 95,
     106, 107, 129, 145, 161, 176
Macdonald, Colin* 96
Macdonald, George* 74
Macdonald, Iain Lom* 53, 130

MacCaig, Norman* 85, 129
MacColla, Fionn* 117
McGrath, John* 89
MacGregor, Alasdair Alpin* 1, 27, 53, 64, 98, 99, 118, 169
McGregor, James* 43
McIlvanney, William* 130
McIntyre Bard* 170
MacIntyre, Donald* 53
MacIntyre, Duncan Bʼn* 90, 107, 130
McKay, John* 159
Mackay, Rob Donn* 14
MacKean, Charles* 2
Mackenzie, Henry* 53
Mackenzie, R.F.* 107
Mackie, Albert D.* 163
Mackintosh, E.A.* 61
Mackintosh, Sir James* 146
MacLauchlin, John H.* 159
Maclean, Alasdair* 112
Maclean, Calum* 12
Maclean, Sorley* 27, 146
MacLennan, Murdoch* 164
MacMhuirich, Giolla Coluim* 75
Macmillan, Harold 130
MacMillan, Roddy* 38
MacNeil, Robert* 46, 131
Mac an Phearsʃinn, Donnchadh* 54
Macpherson, James* 23
McSporran, Alastair* 159
MacWilliam, Candia* 54
Maitland, Sir Richard* 54
Maitland, Sir Thomas* 107
Marr, Andrew* 128
Marshall, Bruce* 58
Mason, William* 108
Masson, Forbes* 118
Maxton, James* 118, 131
Maxwell, James Clerk* 118
Miller, Hugh* 108
Mitchell, Rhea* 12
Monboddo, Lord* 108

Montgomerie, Alexander* 54
Morison, Roderick* 27, 108
Morley, Robert 43
Morton, Tom* 118
Motherwell, William* 27
Muir, Augustus* 166
Muir, Edwin* 54, 119
Muir, Willa* 72
Mundell, David* 119
Munro, Neil* 20, 44
Murray, Charles* 14
Murray, Chic* 119, 170
Murray, R.F.* 61

N
Nairn, Tom* 85, 108, 131
North, Christopher* 109

O
O'Brien, Father A. 132
Orwell, George 155
Outram, George* 36, 85

P
Pagan, Isobel* 100
Parris, Matthew 124
Paulin, Dorothy Margaret* 170
Peacock, Thomas Love 155
Pearce, Edward 132
Pichot, Amédée 28
Pindar, Peter 12
Pinkerton, John* 91, 109
Pinkerton, Roy M.* 122
Pound, Ezra 119
Powell, Anthony 156
Power, William* 78

R
Ramsay, Allan* 18, 100
Ramsay, E.B.* 95, 136
Rees, Nigel 137
Reid, Alastair* 55, 90
Reid, Jimmy* 170
Reith, Lord* 59

Rhymer, Thomas* 19
Rifkind, Sir Malcolm* 63
Roberts, David* 4
Rodger, Alexander* 146
Rodgers, Charles* 97
Rogers, Samuel 109
Roper, Tony* 64, 65
Rosebery, Lord* 59
Ross, Robin* 119
Rush, Christopher* 59, 75, 119
Ruskin, John 73

S
Saki* 39
Salmond, Alex* 47
Scott, Alexander* 170
Scott, Tom* 86
Scott, Sir Walter* 19, 59, 61, 68,
    70, 86, 90, 95, 136, 160, 170
Scott-Moncrieff, George* 86
Self, Will 120
Sharp, Alan* 28
Sheridan, Richard Brinsley 132
Sheridan, Tommy* 47
Shields, Tom* 160
Skirving, Adam* 164
Smart, Alastair* 110
Smith, Adam* 47, 60
Smith, Ian Crichton* 28, 44, 90,
    163
Smith, Sydney 132, 146, 150, 156
Smith, Sydney Goodsir 39
Smith, W. Gordon* 15, 69, 86,
    110, 160
Smollett, Tobias* 23, 70
Smythe, J.M. 110
Soutar, William* 55, 161
Spark, Muriel* 13, 100, 110, 120
Stamfordham, Lord 132
Steel, Sir David* 71
Stein, Jock* 160
Stevenson, Robert Louis* 2, 39,
    44, 55, 71, 87, 110, 120
Stewart, Andrew* 109
Stratford, Esmé Wingfield 111

Stuart, John Roy* 19
Stuart, Thomas* 120
Sturgeon, Nicola* 133
Sully, Duc de 146
Swift, Jonathan 156
Swinburne, A.C. 13

T
Telford, John* 66
Theroux, Paul 120
Thomson, G. Bruce* 39
Thomson, George Malcolm* 20,
    93
Thomson, James* 87, 147
Torrington, Jeff* 39
Tranter, Nigel* 161
Trocchi, Alexander* 13

U
Urquhart, Sir Thomas* 95

V
Victory, Johnny* 28

W
Walkinshaw, Colin* 47
Wanliss, T.D.* 111
Warner, Gerald* 65, 133
Warrack, John* 3
Watt, Christian* 111, 136, 147
Watt, James* 67
Watt, Lauchlan Maclean* 178
Webster, Alexander* 137
Wedderburn brothers* 87
Weldon, Sir Anthony 44, 120, 150,
    156
Welsh, Irvine* 20, 55, 74, 148,
    160, 170
Wodehouse, P.G. 157
Woods, Pat* 157
Wordsworth, William 3, 112, 122
Worsthorne, Peregrine 112

Z
Zangwill, Israel 3